SELECTIVE SECURITY
War and the United Nations
Security Council since 1945

ADAM ROBERTS AND DOMINIK ZAUM

ADELPHI PAPER 395

The International Institute for Strategic Studies

Arundel House | 13–15 Arundel Street | Temple Place | London | WC2R 3DX | UK

ADELPHI PAPER 395

First published June 2008 by **Routledge**
4 Park Square, Milton Park, Abingdon, Oxon, OX14 4RN

for **The International Institute for Strategic Studies**
Arundel House, 13–15 Arundel Street, Temple Place, London, WC2R 3DX, UK
www.iiss.org

Simultaneously published in the USA and Canada by **Routledge**
270 Madison Ave., New York, NY 10016

Routledge is an imprint of Taylor & Francis, an Informa Business

© 2008 The International Institute for Strategic Studies

DIRECTOR-GENERAL AND CHIEF EXECUTIVE John Chipman
EDITOR Tim Huxley
MANAGER FOR EDITORIAL SERVICES Ayse Abdullah
ASSISTANT EDITOR Katharine Fletcher
PRODUCTION John Buck
COVER IMAGE (©AP) US soldier from KFOR at a UN checkpoint on the Kosovo–
Serbia border, February 2008, demolished by Kosovo Serbs after Kosovo's
independence declaration. For over a decade, Kosovo confronted the Security
Council with divisive choices, and in 2007/08 the Council failed to agree on a
solution to its status. Kosovo's unilateral declaration was recognised by the US and
most EU and NATO states, but opposed by Serbia, Russia and other states.

Printed and bound in Great Britain by Bell & Bain Ltd, Thornliebank, Glasgow

British Library Cataloguing in Publication Data
A catalogue record for this book is available from the British Library

Library of Congress Cataloging in Publication Data
A catalogue record for this book is available from the Library of Congress

ISBN 978-0-415-47472-6
ISSN 0567-932X

Contents

Reform

GLOSSARY

AMIS	African Union Mission in Sudan
AMISOM	African Union Mission in Somalia
CIS	Commonwealth of Independent States (ex-Soviet republics)
DRC	Democratic Republic of the Congo
ECOMOG	ECOWAS Ceasefire Monitoring Group (Liberia)
ECOMIL	ECOWAS Multinational Force in Liberia
ECOWAS	Economic Community of West African States
ETA	Euskadi Ta Askatasuna (armed Basque separatist organisation)
EUFOR	European Union Force (in Bosnia; the DRC; and Central African Republic/Chad)
G77	Group of 77 (representing developing countries at the UN)
ICC	International Criminal Court
ICJ	International Court of Justice
IFOR	Implementation Force (in Bosnia)
INTERFET	International Force in East Timor
ISAF	International Security Assistance Force (in Afghanistan)
KFOR	Kosovo Force
MICECI	ECOWAS Mission in Côte d'Ivoire
MIF	Multinational Interim Force (Haiti)
MINUCI	United Nations Mission in Côte D'Ivoire
MINUGUA	United Nations Verification Mission in Guatemala
MINURCAT	United Nations Mission in the Central African Republic
MINUSTAH	United Nations Stabilisation Mission in Haiti
MISAB	Inter-African Mission to Monitor the Implementation of the Bangui Agreements (in Central African Republic)
MNF	Multinational Force (in Iraq; and Haiti)
MONUC	United Nations Organisation Mission in the Democratic Republic of the Congo
MPF	Multinational Protection Force (in Albania)

NPT	Nuclear Non-Proliferation Treaty
ONUC	United Nations Operation in the Congo
ONUSAL	United Nations Observer Mission to El Salvador
P5	The five permanent members of the Security Council
PSI	Proliferation Security Initiative
SFOR	Stabilisation Force (in Bosnia)
UNAMET	United Nations Assistance Mission in East Timor
UNAMID	United Nations–African Union Mission in Darfur
UNAMIR	United Nations Assistance Mission in Rwanda
UNAMSIL	United Nations Mission in Sierra Leone
UNEF	United Nations Emergency Force (in the Middle East)
UNFICYP	United Nations Peacekeeping Force in Cyprus
UNGCI	United Nations Guards Contingent in Iraq
UNITA	National Union for the Total Independence of Angola
UNITAF	Unified Task Force (in Somalia)
UNMEE	United Nations Mission in Ethiopia and Eritrea
UNMIH	United Nations Mission in Haiti
UNMIK	United Nations Interim Administration Mission in Kosovo
UNMIL	United Nations Mission in Liberia
UNMOVIC	United Nations Monitoring, Verification, and Inspection Commission (in Iraq)
UNOCI	United Nations Operation in Côte d'Ivoire
UNOSOM I	United Nations Operation in Somalia
UNOSOM II	Second United Nations Operation in Somalia
UNPREDEP	United Nations Preventive Deployment Force (in Macedonia)
UNPROFOR	United Nations Protection Force (in former Yugoslavia)
UNSCOM	United Nations Special Commission (in Iraq)
UNSCR	United Nations Security Council Resolution
UNTAC	United Nations Transitional Authority in Cambodia
UNTAES	United Nations Transitional Authority in Eastern Slavonia, Baranja, and Western Sirmium (in Croatia)
UNTAET	United Nations Transitional Administration in East Timor
UNTAG	United Nations Transition Assistance Group (in Namibia)
WMD	weapons of mass destruction

INTRODUCTION

The United Nations Security Council is often seen as being, actually or potentially, the key institution in an international system of collective security. Yet the record of the Security Council since its creation in 1945 is one of selectivity. Throughout its history, the Council has frequently been seen to be selective in the crises in which it has become involved and in the actions it has taken. In the Cold War, its members could agree on policies regarding certain peripheral conflicts, but not on most of the serious wars and crises in which the superpowers were involved. Since the end of the Cold War, a more complex pattern of selectivity has emerged, in which the Council has become deeply involved in certain conflicts, such as in the former Yugoslavia and Iraq, but has had a very marginal role in crises, certainly no less serious, in the Israeli-occupied territories, Rwanda and Sudan. It has hardly been involved at all in certain wars and crises of the post-Cold War era, including those in Chechnya and the India–Pakistan 'Kargil War'.

This record suggests that the UN embodies a set of procedures and practices which might be called 'selective security'. That is to say, although the UN provides a framework for states to collectively address, and take action on, certain wars and crises, it does not – indeed cannot – do so for all. The factors that compel the Security Council to be selective include not only the veto power wielded by the Permanent Five (P5) members, but also the limited willingness of all states – whether or not members of the Council – to provide resources and trained personnel to resolve conflicts that they may perceive as distant, complex and resistant to outside involvement. Indeed, in a number of conflicts, the states involved have been reluctant to refer the issue to the Security Council; and many crises are perceived, by some actors at least, as best handled by regional bodies rather than by the UN. The fact that the Council's role is selective does not mean that it has not had an important range of effects on the international system as a whole. Among such effects have been those achieved by its action against clear acts of aggression in Korea in 1950 and Kuwait in 1990, and its provision of peacekeeping forces in a notably wide variety of circumstances.

The selectivity of the Council's performance is generally seen as a problem, and as a challenge to its legitimacy. Indeed, there are several distinct critiques of the UN that revolve around the idea of selectivity. Perhaps the most prevalent is the view of the UN as dominated by the United States, able to act only when the US has an interest, not only in the issue at stake, but in the UN's involvement in it. In this view, the Security Council's involvement in Haiti on the one hand, and its failure to fully engage in Rwanda on the other, merely reflect US interests. A counterpoint to this critique is the view, prevalent in the US, of the Council as failing to address key crises because of the political and economic interests of other permanent member states: the Council's inability to agree on the status of Kosovo in the discussions since 2006 and its failure to agree on stricter sanctions against Iran over uranium enrichment in the same period are cited as instances of this tendency. Further, the Council is often accused of another form of selectivity – being reluctant to involve itself in crises within states even when appalling human-rights violations are taking place: Cambodia under the Khmer Rouge in the 1970s, the wars in the African Great Lakes region following the Rwanda genocide in 1994, and Darfur since 2003 are commonly cited examples.

Although selectivity is often viewed critically, its practice reflects the political realities within which the Council acts, whereby the permanent members and their right to the veto, and the interests and policies of the wider membership of the UN, force the Council to act selectively. Regarding the latter, there have been instances, including several wars and crises in sub-Saharan Africa since the Cold War, in which the Security Council was in principle willing to act, yet member states were not willing to provide the forces needed. All member states have in their different ways been selective in their criticisms, and approvals, of military intervention.

This paper argues the case for taking selectivity seriously in the following steps. Chapter 1 presents a case that, ever since the UN Charter was drawn up in 1945, selectivity has been part of the UN framework, and has been an unavoidable feature of the actions of the UN Security Council and of all UN member states. Chapter 2 begins by outlining changes in the incidence and types of war that have come about over the past decades. It considers the ways in which the Security Council has and has not responded to these changes, recognising that the UN's actions have had some unanticipated and paradoxical effects on the conduct of war. It also notes that in the UN era, partly in response to changes in the character of war, three distinct types of Council-mandated operation have emerged: UN peacekeeping; UN-led institutions, missions and forces not classified as peacekeeping operations; and UN-authorised uses of force by other bodies. The Council has mandated many different states, alliances and international organisations to head UN-authorised uses of force, and certain problems that have resulted from this subcontracting of the direction of force are outlined here. Chapter 3 surveys the long succession of proposals for making standing forces permanently available to the UN Security Council and subject to its direction. It concludes that these proposals have always run into the same obstacle: member states, large and small, are not willing to make forces available unconditionally to the Security Council; and the essentially modest Standby Arrangements System, which permits states a degree of selectivity over how their forces are used, may be the best that can be achieved. Chapter 4 suggests that in the post-Cold War period the UN has tackled, often innovatively, a range of issues relating to the management of force: the expansion of peacekeeping, both quantitatively and qualitatively; the international administration of territories emerging from misrule and conflict; recognition of a greatly expanded range of threats; and the application of the laws of war. In all these matters, innovation has gone hand-in-hand with selectivity. Chapter 5 addresses questions of particular importance in a selective system. How good are the procedures and systems of accountability? What controls exist over the Security Council's policies? Should the Council be enlarged, bearing in mind its unavoidably selective role? The chapter also considers proposals for alternatives to the UN. Finally, the conclusion summarises the weaknesses and the strengths in the Security Council's record, and addresses the implications for states of the understanding of selective security outlined here.

CHAPTER ONE

The Inherent Selectivity of the Council's Roles

The UN Charter system provides a much more robust framework for collective action than any previous attempt at global order. It differs hugely from all its predecessors, including the Concert of Europe in the nineteenth century and the League of Nations in the interwar years. As a result, it has often been asserted that the Charter represents a scheme for collective security.[1] However, we question whether the Charter, even in theory, provides the basis for such a system, at least if defined in the classical sense.

The term 'collective security', in its classical sense, refers to a system, regional or global, in which each state in the system accepts that the security of one is the concern of all, and agrees to join in a collective response to threats to, and breaches of, the peace.[2] This is the meaning followed here. The assumption is that the threats to be addressed may arise from one or more states within the system. Collective security as defined here is distinct from, and more ambitious than, systems of alliance security or collective defence, in which groups of states ally with each other, principally against possible external threats.

There is a long history of the armed forces of many different states being used in a common cause. There is also a distinguished pedigree of leaders who have sought to establish a system of collective security, viewing it as superior to the balance of power as a basis for international order. Cardinal Richelieu of France proposed such a scheme in 1629, and his ideas were partially reflected in the 1648 Peace of Westphalia.[3] Sadly, the history of proposals for collective security is a long record of failure.[4]

Selectivity in the Charter

While the UN Charter has collective-security elements, it can better be read as providing a framework for selectivity on the part of the Security Council. In the Charter scheme, the Security Council has primary, but not exclusive, responsibility for the maintenance of international peace and security.[5] The Council is tasked with determining on behalf of the UN membership whether particular events or activities constitute a threat to international peace and security, and for authorising the use of sanctions and force in a wide range of situations. As Article 24(1) puts it:

> In order to ensure prompt and effective action by the United Nations, its Members confer on the Security Council primary responsibility for the maintenance of international peace and security, and agree that in carrying out its duties under this responsibility the Security Council acts on their behalf.

Remarkably, Article 25 of the Charter, like some articles in Chapter VII, specifies that UN members accept an obligation to do the Security Council's bidding: it is here that the Charter comes closest to a vision of collective security. However, there are also many Charter provisions suggesting a more selective role for the Security Council. Six are outlined below.

The veto

The power of veto, conferred on the P5 by the Charter, is by no means the only factor providing for selectivity on the part of the Security Council, but it is certainly the best known and the most controversial. Charter Article 27, on voting, gives each of the P5 members a veto power. As the article delicately puts it, Council decisions on matters that are not procedural 'shall be made by an affirmative vote of nine members including the concurring votes of the permanent members'.[6] When the great powers discussed the creation of a new world organisation at Dumbarton Oaks in 1944, they agreed on the veto provision so as to guarantee that no military action could be authorised that they did not endorse. Smaller states accepted this to ensure the participation of the great powers in the organisation. The veto power of the P5 has been the subject of controversy throughout the history of the UN.

Table 1 shows that the veto has been used extensively since 1945, especially in the first and fourth decades of the UN's existence, and that its use declined dramatically following the end of the Cold War. Particularly during the Cold War, but also to a lesser extent after it, the use of the veto prevented the Council from taking action on issues in which one or more of the P5

Table 1: **Vetoes cast, vetoed resolutions and resolutions passed in the UN Security Council, 1946–2007**								
	Vetoes cast						Total number of vetoed resolutions	Total number of resolutions passed
Years	China	France	USSR/ Russia	United Kingdom	United States	Total number of vetoes cast		
1946–55	1	2	75	0	0	78	77	110
1956–65	0	2	26	3	0	31	29	108
1966–75	2	2	7	8	12	31	24	165
1976–85	0	9	6	11	34	60	41	196
1986–95	0	3	2	8	24	37	26	455
1996–2005	2	0	1	0	10	13	13	616
2006–07	1	0	1	0	2	4	3	144
TOTAL	**6**	**18**	**118**	**30**	**82**	**254**	**213**	**1794**

Sources: UK Foreign and Commonwealth Office, United Nations

wanted to limit international involvement. Even when the veto is not actually used, it still casts a shadow. In the case of Darfur, a Chinese veto threat for a long time limited the measures authorised by the Security Council, while in the case of Kosovo, the threat of a Russian veto ensured that the Council was not able to resolve the question of the territory's political and legal status.

One attempt to get around the immobilism induced by the P5 veto was the 'Uniting for Peace' resolution passed by the General Assembly in November 1950, which made provision for the General Assembly to act in certain crises or wars when a veto prevented Council action.[7] It came about as a US-led response to the possibility that the Soviet Union might veto the continuation of UN authorisation of the US-led forces in the Korean War. The resolution provides that the General Assembly can call an emergency special session to discuss a crisis, and make recommendations. Since the Korean War, the 'Uniting for Peace' procedure has been invoked 11 times: seven times by the Security Council, and four times by the General Assembly.[8] The resolution has been employed to request the creation of a UN peacekeeping mission (UNEF, during the Suez crisis in 1956) and to confirm the mandate of a mission (ONUC in the Congo in 1960). It has been used to condemn armed interventions (in Suez and Hungary in 1956, Lebanon and Jordan in 1958, Afghanistan in 1980 and the Golan Heights in 1982) and to call for ceasefires (in the Suez crisis and the 1971 India–Pakistan War). It has been invoked to promote decolonisation in Namibia (1981). It has been used, by both the Security Council and the General Assembly, to condemn some of Israel's policies in the Occupied Territories (on various occasions since 1980, most recently in April 2007), and to ask for an advisory opinion from the International Court of Justice (ICJ) on the legality of the construction of a wall by Israel in the West Bank.[9] Significant as this range of activities under the 'Uniting for Peace' procedure is, it does not change the fact that the Security Council veto continues to be the most visible and serious of the many factors that inhibit UN action.

The Council's discretion

Selectivity is inherent in the provisions of Chapter VI (Arts 33–8) of the Charter, which addresses the peaceful settlement of disputes, and Chapter VII (Arts 39–51), which sets out the Council's powers to act in the face of threats to international peace and security. In contrast to the ambiguous language of the League of Nations Covenant, the Charter seeks to identify a single agent – namely the Council – as holding the power to interpret the implications of disputes, conflicts and crises. In its role as maintainer of international peace and security, the Council is empowered by Article 39 of the Charter 'to determine the existence of any threat to the peace, breach of the peace, or act of aggression' and to 'make recommendations, or decide what measures shall be taken … to maintain or restore international peace and security'. Crucially, the Charter sets no limits on the discretion of the Council to make a determination under Article 39.

This right to act selectively was deliberately maintained during the drafting of the Charter: proposals to include detailed definitions of threats to international peace and security, in order to constrain the Council, were defeated. The Council is therefore not tied to any particular legal notion, such as aggression, in making its determinations. Proposals to define and apply terms such as aggression, and efforts to make Council action obligatory in particular circumstances, were driven by small states' concerns that the Council would fail to act.[10] By contrast, since the end of the Cold War, the Council has determined with increased frequency that even events internal to a single state threaten international peace and security.[11] Indeed, some states are now uneasy with the growing scope of the Council's actions. While in the past the Council made most of its determinations in relation to specific crises and threats, more recently it has done so in relation to general threats, for example in its resolutions in 2001 and 2004 on terrorist acts and on nuclear non-proliferation.[12]

The breadth of the Council's discretion to decide what triggers its powers under Chapters VI and VII is mirrored by the breadth of those powers themselves. Unlike that of member states, the Council's right to use force is not limited to situations of self-defence. If it wished to initiate preventive military action in order to avert a threat to international peace and security, it could do so. Chapter VII gives the Security Council the right to use 'measures not involving the use of force' (Art. 41), such as economic sanctions or the severance of diplomatic relations, to maintain international peace and security; it also provides the right to use force 'should the Security Council consider that measures provided for in Article 41 would be inadequate or have proved to be inadequate'.[13] Thus there is no necessity for the Council to try sanctions before resorting to force: it is up to the Council to select the appropriate instrument.

Selective implementation of decisions

The Charter also recognises that the implementation by states of Security Council decisions might sometimes be selective and, for example, be undertaken by a limited number of states. Article 48(1), by specifying that some actions may be taken by groups of states rather than the membership as a whole, provides a basis for the Council's later practice: 'The action required to carry out the decisions of the Security Council for the maintenance of international peace and security shall be taken by all the Members of the United Nations or by some of them, as the Security Council may determine.'

Inherent right of self-defence

This understanding of the Security Council as the lynchpin of a selective, rather than collective, security system is also underlined by the provisions of Article 51 of the Charter. These make it clear that states have an already existing right of self-defence, which is simply recognised (and not conferred) by the Charter. 'Nothing in the present Charter shall impair the inherent right of individual or collective self-defence if an armed attack occurs against a Member of the United Nations, until the Security Council has taken measures necessary to maintain international peace and security.' Importantly, while the article recognises the right of the Council to take action in such cases, there is no obligation on it to do so. There is no presumption in the Charter that the Security Council offers a complete alternative security system replacing that of states or groups of states.

Regional arrangements

The Charter recognises that the Security Council cannot tackle all problems of peace and security alone, but will have to be selective and at times act together with regional security arrangements. The key issue of how the UN and regional security arrangements might coexist and even reinforce each other was discussed extensively in the Dumbarton Oaks negotiations, partly in recognition of the fact that not every international security problem could be addressed at the global level. Article 52(1) of the Charter states:

> Nothing in the present Charter precludes the existence of regional arrangements or agencies for dealing with such matters relating to the maintenance of international peace and security as are appropriate for regional action, provided that such arrangements or agencies and their activities are consistent with the Purposes and Principles of the United Nations.

Regarding the delicate question of how the Council and regional arrangements should relate to each other, Chapter VIII of the Charter (Articles 52–4) clearly emphasises the primacy of the Council. In particular, it specifies the need for it to authorise any use of force by regional security arrangements, and it imposes an obligation on regional bodies to keep the Council informed of 'activities undertaken or in contemplation'.[14] It is asking a lot of states, and of the Council, to expect these precepts to be followed in all cases, but if the Charter had failed to make such requirements, it would have undermined the primacy of the Council even before it came into existence. In practice, the requirement that the enforcement actions of regional bodies be authorised by the Security Council was little heeded during the Cold War, as there was never much chance of securing both US and Soviet consent for any particular military action by a regional or indeed any other body; but since 1991, many Council resolutions have referred to the military actions of regional organisations.[15]

Relations between the UN and NATO in particular have been complex in this regard. Throughout the Cold War, NATO sought to emphasise its role as a collective defence alliance, rather than a regional body, within the meaning of the UN Charter, so as to make clear that it was not bound by the obligations to keep the Council informed of planned activities and to seek Council authorisation for the use of force, which would have subjected it to the threat of a Soviet veto in the Council. Since the end of the Cold War, however, NATO has regularly acted as a regional organisation on behalf of the Security Council, in particular in the former Yugoslavia.

The relationship between the UN and regional bodies has proved to be more varied than was envisaged in 1945. Increasingly, regional bodies have acted with Council approval outside their own region, for example NATO in Afghanistan since January 2002 and the EU in the Democratic Republic of the Congo (DRC) in 2006. Furthermore, Council resolutions have given retrospective approval to certain actions of regional bodies, for example the endorsement of the intervention in Liberia by the Economic Community of West African States (ECOWAS) in 1990.

At times, the Council has also authorised regional bodies to operate alongside a UN peacekeeping operation: a prime example of this is in Kosovo, where NATO-led KFOR troops have been responsible for maintaining peace and security, while the UN Interim Administration Mission in Kosovo (UNMIK), although it is formally classified as a UN peacekeeping operation, has been mainly concerned with its responsibilities for policing, institution-building and governance. In Darfur, the Council has gone one step further and established for the first time a 'hybrid' peacekeeping force (UNAMID) under the joint control of the UN and a regional body, in this case the African Union.

There are solid reasons for the increased reliance on regional bodies to address security problems. Some regional bodies and alliances have, or plan to have, forces available and a capacity to act promptly that the UN conspicuously lacks. The ability of certain regional forces to operate outside as well as within their own region is particularly striking. Moreover, the post-1945 tendency for civil wars to be among the principal problems of international relations poses a problem for the Security Council. It is not obvious that there is a strong global interest in addressing every civil war, nor that the UN has the appropriate resources at its disposal to do so. There has to be selectivity in determining which conflicts to address at a global level, regionally, or in combination.

The 'enemy states' provisions

Finally, Articles 53 and 107 left each of the wartime Allies a free hand to handle their relations with Second World War enemy states outside the Charter framework. These articles were a significant concession to unilateralism in the conduct of the post-war occupations, but they have been a dead letter for many years, and the World Summit of September 2005 proposed the deletion from the Charter of references to 'enemy states'.[16]

Not a collective security system

Although the Charter is not a blueprint for a general system of classically defined collective security, it may be compatible with a looser definition of collective security. In the 1990s, US diplomat James Goodby suggested that classical definitions had been 'too narrowly constructed to be a practical guide to policy analysis, especially when considering the use of military force'. He therefore proposed a definition of collective security as 'a policy that commits governments to develop and enforce broadly accepted international rules and to seek to do so through collective action legitimized by representative international organisations'.[17] While this less stringent conception of collective security better captures how some states responded to war and other threats to peace and security in the post-1945 period, not only through the Security Council, but also through other bodies, including NATO, it is doubtful whether it adds up to a system for providing security.

Nonetheless, in 2004, the UN High-level Panel Report on Threats, Challenges and Change placed heavy emphasis on the proposition that what the UN must aim to establish is a 'collective security system':

> The central challenge for the twenty-first century is to fashion a new and broader understanding, bringing together all these strands, of what collective security means – and of all the responsibilities, commitments, strategies and institutions that come with it if a collective security system is to be effective, efficient and equitable.[18]

The High-level Panel report used the term 'collective security system' in an innovative way, to refer to a UN-centred system of international security that addressed a notably wide range of threats. The panel sought to advance within a UN framework a broad view of security policy as addressing the problems of terrorism, nuclear proliferation and state breakdown, as well as more conventional security threats; and it indicated the possibility of building, on this basis, a common international approach to security issues.

However, there were risks associated with the report's use of the concept of 'collective security' as a benchmark for assessing the performance and potential of the Security Council. The concept inevitably brings to mind memories of unhappy episodes (including in the years 1919–39) in which failed attempts were made to create such systems. It is not an accident that, in the wake of this bitter experience, the term 'collective security' was not used in the UN Charter. The use of the term has contributed to the outcome that the High-level Panel report, like *An Agenda for Peace* in 1992, with its proposals for a remarkably extensive UN role in the security sphere, has come to be seen as hopelessly optimistic: as purporting to set up a general security system though in reality the UN, while it can perform a large number of useful security functions, cannot hope to constitute anything as ambitious as that. In addition, the emphasis on 'collective security' may have obscured some notable elements of realism in the report, including its frank recognition of the continuing role of states as 'front-line actors in dealing with all the threats, new and old'.

The idea of the Charter as a recipe for collective security is potentially damaging to the UN. It provides fodder to critics who hold the organisation to that high standard. It also encourages a line of argument which sees the Charter framework as a completely valid collective security scheme that would have been effective but for the faults and failures of particular states. This line has corrosive political consequences, as blame is attached to a few states and individuals for weaknesses in the UN system that are in fact the result of deep and enduring problems of world politics.

A dose of scepticism about the UN's transformative ambitions is healthy. Peter Marshall, a former British diplomat who served at the UN, once proposed a new Article 112 to conclude the Charter: 'Nothing in the present Charter should be allowed to foster the illusion that power is no longer of any consequence.'[19] However, the fact that the UN has not lived up to the highest hopes held out for it does not mean that it has had no effect on the management of international security and the conduct of power politics. What it has offered is a contribution to security, albeit a thoroughly selective one.

Selectivity and impartiality

Impartiality is not mentioned in the Charter, but the idea of impartiality as a fundamental principle of UN operations has become deeply embedded in much thought and writing about the UN. The term has been used in particular in connection with peacekeeping operations, its traditional meaning amounting to 'neutrality between the parties to a conflict'. But this approach has come under considerable stress, first in Congo in the early 1960s, and then in many conflicts in the post-Cold War period. In particular, the inaction of small and vulnerable UN peacekeeping forces when faced with genocide in Rwanda in 1994 and the mass killings at Srebrenica in Bosnia in 1995 forced many to rethink the impartiality principle. In 2000, the Brahimi Report on UN peace operations stated succinctly:

> The Panel concurs that consent of the local parties, impartiality and the use of force only in self-defence should remain the bedrock principles of peacekeeping. Experience shows, however, that in the context of intra-State/transnational conflicts, consent may be manipulated in many ways. Impartiality for United Nations operations must therefore mean adherence to the principles of the Charter: where one party to a peace agreement clearly and incontrovertibly is violating its terms, continued equal treatment of all parties by the United Nations can in the

best case result in ineffectiveness and in the worst may amount to complicity with evil. No failure did more to damage the standing and credibility of United Nations peacekeeping in the 1990s than its reluctance to distinguish victim from aggressor.[20]

The core weakness of rigid applications of the principle of impartiality by the Security Council is that they undermine selectivity in its best sense – that is, making clear moral and strategic decisions about the causes of conflict and the most appropriate response. In particular, in civil wars in which merely freezing the status quo is rarely a feasible approach, it is sometimes necessary to take firm action against one party or its activities; or to support one side against the other.

The need for selectivity is not confined to cases of peacekeeping. It is also a precondition of much enforcement activity, effective sanctions and post-conflict peace-building. The Security Council is not an impartial judicial body, but a deeply political organisation, to which a selective approach is more appropriate. Impartiality remains important in certain operations, and elements of impartiality must necessarily continue to be a guide to the Council in ensuring that its decision-making is seen to be fair and reasonable. Selectivity itself is only perceived as legitimate if it is based on procedural and substantive fairness.

The Council as an instrument of powerful states

The Security Council is often viewed, and criticised, as a mere instrument of powerful states. Certainly one of its intended functions, reflected in the provisions of the Charter, is to provide for structured collaboration between the major powers. This framework raises a number of questions. First, to what extent, in the various periods of the UN's history, has such collaboration actually occurred? Second, has the Council provided a vehicle for the continuation of patterns of great-power dominance, such as through the acceptance of spheres of influence? Third, has the US in particular enjoyed unparalleled dominance of the Council, including through special influence over other members of the Council? Fourth, have perceptions of great-power dominance corroded the Council's authority?

It is often said that in the Cold War the Council could not perform its intended function of facilitating cooperation between the major powers, in particular the P5. However, rivalry between the Soviet Union and the US and its allies did not always prevent collaboration. Both inside and outside the Security Council, there was a measure of agreement on such matters as nuclear proliferation, the principle if not always the practice of decolonisation, and the establishment of certain peacekeeping operations. But this modest degree of great-power cooperation was not always for the benefit of states or peoples in crisis, nor was it always easy to square with principles enunciated in the Charter. For example, in the Iran–Iraq War of 1980–8, as discussed further below, the P5 members chose collectively not to act decisively against Iraq, despite the evidence of Iraqi aggression; and individually their actions tended to show partiality in favour of Iraq.

Since the end of the Cold War, the Council has been significantly more active than before, and in a wide variety of ways. It has set up numerous peacekeeping operations, authorised force in a broad range of circumstances, and become involved in the governance of post-conflict states and the establishment of criminal tribunals. All this attests to a degree of cooperation between powerful states, especially the P5 members. However, there have been clear limits to the extent of this great-power cooperation. In respect of many crises, there has neither been agreement on the nature of the problem nor on the actions to be taken to address it.

The dominance of great powers in international politics is reflected in the continuation in the UN era of a much older method of managing international order – through spheres of influence. In some ways, the Charter provisions regarding the Council have actually assisted this continuation. In particular, the existence of the right of veto has in most cases enabled the P5 to prevent Council action in regard to crises in which they have a direct interest. For example, in the Cold War years, the Council was inactive over the many crises and interventions involving the Soviet Union and its Eastern European satellites; over US interventions in Cuba in 1961 and Grenada in 1983; and over France's various interventions in its former colonies in Africa. In the post-Cold War period, the Council has had very varied degrees of involvement with interventions by major powers in countries traditionally seen to lie within their spheres of influence. It has had a notably limited and cautious relationship with the largely Russian CIS[21] peacekeeping mission in the Abkhaz breakaway region of Georgia since 1994, in contrast, it authorised the US-led intervention in Haiti in 1994 and the French intervention in Côte d'Ivoire in 2003. The undoubted need for some form of intervention in a range of conflicts, and the perennial difficulty of mobilising the necessary military resources, suggest that spheres of influence, and the concomitant willingness of powerful states to take on a leadership role within them, fulfil an important, if controversial, function with regard to international order. The involvement of the Council can help to contain some of the unilateralism associated with such spheres, by tying interventions to specified purposes, involving a wider range of states in providing personnel, and subjecting operations to multi-lateral decision-making or oversight.

The widespread perception of US dominance of the Council is based on several observations. Many, but by no means all, UN-authorised military interventions have been conducted under US leadership or (in the case of NATO missions) have had significant US participation. In some cases, its critics have seen the US as securing UN support and legitimacy for action it intended to take in any case, with or without UN support – for example the UN authorisation in October 2003 of a continued foreign presence in Iraq (relabelled the Multinational Force).[22] Furthermore, the US has repeatedly withheld its financial contributions to the UN in order to exert pressure on the organisation to pursue particular reforms, including reduction of the proportion of UN costs borne by the US, and changes to management structures. At the 2005 World Summit, the US tied its payments to the UN budget to a programme of management reforms. While the withholding of dues is not an unusual pressure tactic among member states, the size of US contributions increases its relative impact. The perception of American dominance is also based on the US's extensive use of the veto. Between 1990 and 2007, of a total of 22 vetoes, the US cast 15, the majority of which related to proposed resolutions on the Israel–Palestine conflict. In addition, the US has acted on the Council to secure special exemption for its forces from the attentions of the International Criminal Court (ICC): it vetoed a draft resolution on Bosnia on 30 June 2002 on the grounds that US peace-keepers should be allowed to remain outside the legal framework alluded to in the resolution, then voted in favour of a resolution extending the mandate of the UN Mission in Bosnia and Herzegovina two weeks later, having in a separate resolution on the same day gained immunity from ICC prosecution for its soldiers.[23]

There is also evidence of the US using its economic muscle in attempts to influence other Council members. US aid to non-permanent member countries has been found to increase significantly whilst they are serving on the Council, and to decline as their terms end.[24] It remains an open question whether the distribution of such largesse inspires either gratitude or compliance. In the run-up to the 2003 Iraq War, despite intense lobbying and arm-twisting, the US conspicuously failed to gather support from the non-permanent members sufficient to give it any prospect of mustering a majority of votes for the invasion.

Perceptions of dominance of the international system by a single power, or by a small number of states, are of course nothing new, and they often involve over-simplifications of a much more complex reality. Yet they can cause profound damage. In the case of the UN Security Council, they can result in non-compliance with the terms of certain resolutions, and also in a tendency on the part of states to look elsewhere (including to regional bodies) for possible security frameworks.

The pursuit of international order outside the UN framework

While the UN Charter does not claim a monopoly for the UN on managing international order, it does contain a vision of an international system in which the organisation has a central role. In practice, though, the UN system has always operated alongside other institutions and other means of addressing key international order issues.

One example is disarmament and arms control – a field in which both the Security Council and the General Assembly have responsibilities under the Charter. Each body has passed numerous resolutions on armaments and disarmament: indeed, the first resolution passed by either body was a General Assembly resolution on control of atomic weapons.[25] Several important agencies concerned with disarmament, including the International Atomic Energy Agency, which was established in 1957, have a close association with the UN. The UN has a long record of organising conferences on disarmament, some of which have contributed to significant agreements, including the 1968 Treaty on the Non-Proliferation of Nuclear Weapons (NPT) and the 1993 Chemical Weapons Convention. Yet many UN conferences in this area have been unproductive. At the same time, several arms-control and disarmament agreements have been concluded largely outside the UN framework. Examples include the 1963 Partial Nuclear Test Ban Treaty, the 1972 US–Soviet Strategic Arms Limitation Accords and the 1987 US–Soviet Agreement on the Elimination of Intermediate-range Missiles. In these cases, reasons for negotiating outside a UN framework included the view, taken by the United States and the Soviet Union, that the rest of the world did not have the necessary *locus standi* to co-determine how the two superpowers should agree between themselves to manage their arsenals. There was also concern about the tendency of large multilateral conferences to be stronger on rhetoric, and on sticking to well-established principles and policies, than on getting down to deals.

Similarly, some effective negotiations on regional problems have been conducted outside a UN framework. For example, on Arab–Israeli issues, and on southern Africa in the apartheid years, negotiations under UN auspices were encumbered by the fact that they tended to involve so many countries, and were somewhat constrained, diplomatically, by the clear stances on the regions' problems expressed in General Assembly resolutions – especially those condemning Israel's occupation of neighbouring territories and the continuation of white minority rule in South Africa. Thus in both cases, certain key negotiations took place outside a UN framework, often with the US rather than the UN as a key broker. A defining characteristic of many such negotiations has been the mixture of UN and extra-UN activity, with the UN regularly laying down the guiding principles, helping to keep the parties to them, and then acting as the rallying point in gathering political support for the end result.

In general, the era since 1945 has witnessed – alongside the new institution of the United Nations and the multilateral diplomacy that it embodies – the continuation of all the classical institutions of the international system: great powers, alliances, spheres of interest, balances of power and bilateral diplomacy. Even the most questionable of international institutions, war and threats of war, continue to have some place in the relations of states.

Selectivity, the Council and nuclear proliferation

One international security issue on which Security Council selectivity has been particularly evident is nuclear proliferation. The NPT did not foresee an active role for the Security Council. However, the issue of possession of nuclear weapons, and efforts to counter their proliferation, have become closely associated with the Council. The NPT recognises as nuclear powers only those states that exploded a nuclear device before 1 January 1967.[26] Since the admission of the People's Republic of China to the UN in 1971, these have been the P5. The view seems to have taken hold among many states that permanent membership in the Council is inextricably linked to recognition as a nuclear power. This view may have contributed to the ambition of some states aspiring to permanent membership to acquire nuclear weapons, with damaging consequences for the non-proliferation regime.

The fact that only a few powers are accepted under the NPT as being entitled to possess nuclear weapons creates particular tensions. Many states have interpreted the treaty as requiring extensive or even total nuclear disarmament by the P5, seeing such disarmament as the quid pro quo for their continuing acceptance of the treaty. When the NPT was extended indefinitely at the NPT Review Conference in 1995, the P5 made limited commitments to further nuclear disarmament. Similarly limited commitments were made at the 2005 Review Conference. The legitimacy of the regime, and the privileges it grants to the P5, have increasingly come under challenge.[27] The comment made by Jaswant Singh, adviser to then-Prime Minister of India Atal Behari Vajpayee, soon after India under-took nuclear tests in 1998, summarises a commonly held position: 'If the permanent five continue to employ nuclear weapons as an international currency of force and power, why should India voluntarily devalue its own state power and national security?'.[28]

However, this 'disarmament view' of the NPT as a deal whereby the P5 promise to disarm in return for the restraint of other powers is histori-cally questionable and politically damaging. It ignores both the extent to which the NPT was also a bargain between *non*-nuclear states to provide mutual reassurance that proliferation would be avoided, and the nego-tiators' recognition that some states would retain their nuclear weapons. Disarmament specialist Joachim Krause has vigorously criticised the disar-mament view of the NPT deal:

> One might even argue that international order – defined as the rule of non-use of force – is possible only when a small number of responsible states possess nuclear weapons. The issue is, however, how to keep problematic actors from getting control of nuclear weapons. There is no golden key available to solve this dilemma, but the 1968 NPT was at least a very successful instrument in striking such a deal.[29]

The fact that certain other states beyond the P5 have developed nuclear weapons has also contributed to the revival of questions about the legitimacy and adequacy of the non-proliferation regime. Above all, the problem remains that, although most states agree that non-proliferation is desirable, a convincing rationale for the regime's selectivity, for why certain states should possess nuclear weapons and others not, has proved remarkably elusive.

The NPT has had some notable successes, not least the fact that 190 countries have become parties to it. It has helped to limit the number of nuclear states to – currently – eight or nine. In the 1980s and early 1990s, a range of countries gave up nuclear arsenals (South Africa, Belarus, Kazakhstan and Ukraine) or programmes (Argentina and Brazil). In 2004, Libya ended its programmes for developing weapons of mass destruction (WMD). In none of these cases, however, did the Security Council play a decisive role.

The Council has at times been more active, but also highly selective, with regard to nuclear proliferation. There have been two main approaches. One was the establishment of an inspections regime to monitor the destruc-tion of Iraqi WMD following the 1991 Gulf War, through the UN Special

Commission (UNSCOM, 1991–9) and later the UN Monitoring, Verification and Inspection Commission (UNMOVIC, which operated in Iraq in 2002 and 2003 and remotely after that, as the US-led coalition in Iraq was not willing to see its return).[30] The regime was fatally undermined by Iraqi non-compliance, CIA involvement in UNSCOM and, ultimately, the erroneous US perception that UNMOVIC provided insufficient safeguards against the possibility of Iraq's acquisition of WMD. The Council's other major counter-proliferation effort comprised the sanctions regimes designed to enforce disarmament in Iraq and put pressure on North Korea and Iran to end their nuclear programmes.[31] The impact of sanctions has been mixed: while they appear to have helped to prevent Saddam Hussein from restart-ing his WMD programme, and may have contributed to the North Korean willingness to sign a de-nuclearisation agreement in February 2007, they seem to have had little effect on the Iranian nuclear programme.

On other proliferation issues, the Council has been more passive. When India and Pakistan tested nuclear devices in May 1998, it merely expressed its concern, urging both states to conduct no further tests and join the NPT.[32] At times, certain P5 governments have been criticised for undermining the provisions of the NPT. Up to the mid 1990s, China technologically and materially supported the development of Pakistan's nuclear programme;[33] and in March 2006, the US government concluded the controversial Civil Nuclear Cooperation Agreement with India that has been viewed by some as assisting proliferation.[34]

The Council and its key member states have been particularly concerned to prevent the proliferation of WMD to terrorists. In April 2004, the Council passed Resolution 1540, requiring states to refrain from supporting non-state actors in their attempts to acquire WMD, and to pass domestic legislation to prevent the proliferation of such weapons. The resolution gave the Council the role of monitoring state efforts in this area and offering assistance, but it did not give it enforcement powers. The Council's activities are complemented by other mechanisms to prevent the trafficking of WMD to terrorists, such as the US-led Proliferation Security Initiative (PSI) to interdict WMD shipments. Not based on a multilateral treaty, and not giving states general legal authority to interdict and board ships, the PSI is comprised of a range of bilateral boarding agreements between the US and large ship-registry states such as Panama and Liberia, which each grant the US authority to interdict and board ships registered in the signatory country.[35]

The non-proliferation issue illustrates two central themes of the Security Council's role. Firstly, it is one of many security issues on which the Council is forced to act selectively: although there is a general interest in controlling nuclear proliferation, there has been no realistic possibility of stopping certain states (e.g., India) from developing a nuclear-weapons capability. Secondly, this is one of many fields in which the Council must necessarily operate alongside states and other international bodies, including alliances and informal arrangements.

The selectivity of states regarding the Security Council

Any discussion of the Council's practices and record needs to recognise that the Council is not a homogeneous corporate entity, but rather a focal point for state cooperation, especially great-power cooperation.[36] Its record is therefore shaped by the preferences and practices of its member states. The selectivity of member states with regard to the Council's efforts to address the problem of war has taken two forms.

Firstly, states are selective when deciding whether or not to seek Council involvement in a conflict.[37] This is not only a matter of P5 members using the veto to prevent the Council from addressing conflicts in which either they or close allies are involved. Other states have either relied on their P5 allies to threaten or use the veto, or have used their own political clout to prevent Council action. In the wars between India and Pakistan, for example, India has generally sought to prevent a greater role for the Council, fearing that Council involvement would be inimical to its interests.[38]

Secondly, states have been partial and selective in their implementation of Security Council resolutions. This tendency has been most pronounced in the context of peacekeeping operations. States have never made forces permanently available to the UN in the manner envisaged in Articles 43 and 45 of the Charter. Instead, in their various standby agreements with the UN, states have retained discretion about when and how their forces are used. As a consequence, peacekeeping operations have at times had insufficient forces for the mandates given to them by the Security Council. General Sir Rupert Smith, commander in 1995 of the UN peacekeeping force in Bosnia, UNPROFOR, has pointed out that although the UN force was tasked in 1993 with helping to protect the 'safe areas' of Srebrenica, Zepa, Gorazde, Sarajevo, Tuzla and Bihac, states were never willing to provide the reinforcements necessary to fulfil this task. Of the additional 34,000 troops that the military planners deemed necessary, only 7,000 arrived – some only late in 1994, almost 18 months after the establishment of the safe areas.[39] In Rwanda, the Security Council belatedly responded to the genocide by expanding the mandate and size of its peacekeeping operation, UNAMIR, in May 1994. However, none of the 19 member states that had agreed to provide peacekeeping troops under the UN's standby arrangements was willing to provide forces for UNAMIR. This situation changed only after the Tutsi-led Rwandan Patriotic Front defeated Rwandan government forces and ended the genocide.[40] Two years later, in November 1996, the Council authorised a Multinational Force for Zaire to facilitate the return of aid agencies to refugee camps in the east of the country,[41] but not enough states were willing to provide sufficient troops, and the force was never deployed.

Underlying reasons for the Council's selectivity

What are the underlying reasons for the selectivity of the Security Council? The Council's selectivity is rooted in the Charter as well as in the political realities within which the Council operates, and it has been reinforced by more than 60 years of practice. The reasons for the divergence from the principle of collective security are deep-seated, and reflect the inherent limitations of an international organisation such as the UN. The existence of the veto is part of the explanation, affecting as it does most areas of the Council's activity and inactivity. But it is not the sole explanation.

A multinational body such as the Security Council is not the most effective wielder of military force. Represented on the Council are very different perspectives on the world and the threats it faces, and the organisation's members at times show varying degrees of commitment to action in a particular crisis. Also, while Article 23 of the Charter asks that the contribution of member states to the maintenance of international peace and security be a criterion for Council membership, this requirement has in practice generally been superseded by a concern to ensure adequate representation on the Council of all regions. Partly because of these factors, the Council has tended to authorise a lead state to manage UN military operations at the head of a coalition, rather than manage the use of force itself, as a classical collective security system would demand. The Council's ability to manage the use of force has also been constrained by the UN's lack of an intelligence system, something that is normally seen as an essential prerequisite for the effective conduct of military operations. The notion of the UN possessing such a system is controversial because of concerns about state sovereignty, and fears that any such system would be dominated by the US.[42] The UN has also never established its own armed forces as envisaged in the Charter. States have generally remained cautious about the circumstances in which their armed forces might be used, and are unwilling to write blank cheques to the UN. In planning the use of armed forces

– whether for enforcement or peacekeeping – the Council has never been able to assume that all states are waiting to do its bidding. It has constantly had to adjust its policies to what member states, and particularly the troop-contributing states, will tolerate.

The changing character of war may have some bearing on member states' caution about troop and resource commitments. The types of war seen since 1945 have been different from the classic scenario of armed aggression by one state against another: most armed conflicts in this period have been civil wars, generally occurring in post-colonial or post-communist states whose frontiers, constitutions and types of political system may not have been accepted as legitimate, either internally or externally. In wars of these types, it may be difficult or impossible to determine which party is the aggressor, and the response that is needed may be very different from collective military action against a presumed aggressor. Thus the response of the international community tends to be to assist a negotiated settlement and to provide peacekeeping forces to observe and aid its implementation. This is a principal reason why peacekeeping, rather than the use of force against offending states, has been the main mode of UN action. Member states are often wary about involvement in such operations, partly because of the opacity and apparent intractability of many civil conflicts, and the open-endedness of the peacekeeping task. Thus the changing character of war could be seen as indirectly contributing to Council selectivity; and as reinforcing the pressures to handle security problems at the regional rather than global level – a possibility already foreshadowed in the UN Charter.

Ultimately, much of the Security Council's selectivity reflects the awkward fact that powerful states, if they are willing to act on behalf of international order, need some recognised latitude in which to do so, and a degree of flexibility regarding when they will act and with what means. This was an important theme in earlier eras, when the rights and duties of the 'great powers' were under debate. It remains relevant in the UN era. To a limited extent, the UN Charter and the international order that has evolved since 1945 recognise that certain states have a special degree of latitude. Yet on numerous points relating to selectivity – authorisations to major powers to act on the UN's behalf, the inevitable discretion used in decisions about whether and how to intervene, certain states' maintenance of nuclear-weapons status while denying it to others, the need to involve more powers than the current P5 in the management of international order – the legitimacy of the present order is continuously in question.

The Council's selectivity also reflects its limited resources. No body and no organisation can enforce all the rules, all the time. They should not even try to do so: law enforcement is expensive, and in all cases a balance has to be struck between tolerable economic and social costs of law enforcement on the one hand and a tolerable degree of law-breaking on the other. The Security Council is no exception to this rule, and it is not useful to criticise it because of its inability to intervene in every situation that arises – although one can, of course, reasonably say that the balance between the costs and benefits of law enforcement has not been struck in the right place. But there is another, related argument that has more force. It is that the Security Council should have a consistent, or at least a rational and defensible, policy on the circumstances in which it will and will not act.

The need for such a policy leads us to the question of the Council's role in the maintenance of the rule of law. Why is action taken against one state but not another? Why, for instance, are Israel and Iran and North Korea treated so differently from each other in the context of nuclear non-proliferation? On the view of justice as the treating of like cases alike, and of the rule of law as the impartial administration of justice, the selectivity of the Council's response may seem to deprive it of credibility as the guarantor of the rule of law in international society.

The short answer to these questions is that the Council is not intended to maintain the rule of law: it was intended to maintain international peace and security. That is a very different, and more limited, role. The Security Council is not a 'world policeman': it is an institutionalised process for managing international crises. Selectivity is an inherent, and prudent, aspect of this role.

CHAPTER TWO

Wars and Crises since 1945: The Overall Record

The Security Council has been involved in an extraordinary range of activities relating to war, from monitoring and mediation to the use of force and long-term reconstruction of political and social institutions after conflict. It has operated in a period in which there have been profound changes in the incidence and character of war, to which it has itself sometimes contributed, and to which it has had to adapt and respond with innovative measures.

In brief, five propositions can be advanced about changes in the incidence and toll of war since 1945:

- The death toll from inter-state war has been lower than in earlier periods.
- There has been a decline in the incidence of inter-state war since the mid 1970s.
- Colonial wars, as fought by European countries in their overseas possessions, declined dramatically following the demise of the European empires in the period from 1945 to the 1970s.
- Since 1945, and especially since the 1970s, a principal form of armed conflict has been civil war or other conflict in which at least one of the parties is not, or not yet, a state. In cases where outside powers become directly involved in such wars, these conflicts can be described as 'internationalised' civil wars.

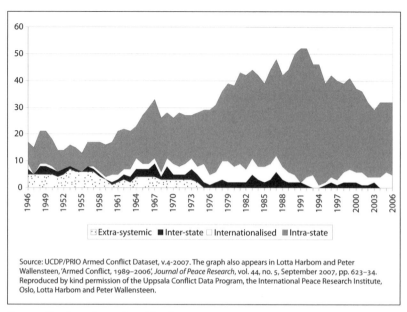

Source: UCDP/PRIO Armed Conflict Dataset, v.4-2007. The graph also appears in Lotta Harbom and Peter Wallensteen, 'Armed Conflict, 1989–2006', *Journal of Peace Research*, vol. 44, no. 5, September 2007, pp. 623–34. Reproduced by kind permission of the Uppsala Conflict Data Program, the International Peace Research Institute, Oslo, Lotta Harbom and Peter Wallensteen.

Figure 1: **Number of armed conflicts by type, 1946–2006**

- The incidence of civil war has declined since the mid 1990s, after peaking after the end of the Cold War and the dissolution of the Soviet Union and the former Yugoslavia.

The inherent problems of the statistical study of war notwithstanding,[1] an impressive number of statistical studies of the incidence of armed conflict support the propositions outlined above. Figure 1 gives a rough illustration of the changes within the period. It shows four types of armed conflict: inter-state armed conflict (war between sovereign states, or 'international' war); 'extra-systemic' armed conflict (colonial war between an indigenous force and an external army); intra-state armed conflict (civil war); and internationalised intra-state armed conflict (civil war in which one side or both receives external support, including the participation of foreign troops).

As Figure 1 suggests, the diminution of international war since the mid 1970s is a long way from amounting to the elimination of war generally. The numerous wars since 1945 have been predominantly civil wars, many of which have seen international involvement on one or both sides. The apparent decline in the incidence of inter-state war since the mid 1970s, and of civil war since the mid 1990s, may or may not continue: there have been periods with a relatively low incidence of war before. Nonetheless, the decline in the number of international wars is striking enough for its causes to be worth investigating.

Causes of the decline of international war

A diminution in the number of international wars is especially noteworthy given that the number of states has reached unprecedented levels in recent decades: at the end of 2007, there were 192 UN member states.

What are the possible explanations for the apparent decline? The *Human Security Report* for 2005 proposed a series of factors to account for the diminution in the incidence of war since the 1980s:

- A dramatic increase in the number of democracies. In 1946, there were 20 democracies in the world; in 2005, there were 88. Many scholars argue that this trend has reduced the likelihood of international war because democratic states almost never fight each other: this is the 'democratic peace' argument.
- An increase in economic interdependence between states. Greater global economic interdependence has increased the costs of cross-border aggression, while significantly reducing its benefits (see point below).
- A decline in the economic utility of war. The most effective path to prosperity in modern economies is through increasing productivity and international trade, not through seizing land and raw materials. In addition, the existence of an open global trading regime means it is nearly always cheaper to buy resources from overseas than to use force to acquire them.

Only after mentioning these factors does the report turn to the growth in international institutions as a possible explanation for the declining trend: 'The greatly increased involvement by governments in international institutions can help reduce the incidence of conflict. Such institutions play an important direct role in building global norms that encourage the peaceful settlement of disputes. They can also benefit security indirectly by helping promote democratisation and interdependence.'[2]

In addition to the explanations for the decline in inter-state war noted by the *Human Security Report*, there are other important possibilities. Firstly, the UN era has coincided with the nuclear age. On 16 July 1945, just three weeks after the signing of the UN Charter, the US tested the first atomic bomb; in 1949 the Soviet Union followed suit. While it involved terrible risks, the incorporation of nuclear weapons into the armouries of the major powers, and the gradual emergence of a situation of mutual assured destruction, undoubtedly introduced an element of caution into relations between these powers – and also into the policies of some of their allies. This critically important development overlapped with the role of the UN Security Council – not least because, from 1971 onwards, the five recognised nuclear powers were also the five permanent members of the Council, tasked with maintaining world peace and security. However, subsequently, the development of nuclear weapons by Israel, India, Pakistan, North Korea and others indicated that the vision of the Security Council permanent members as forming the club of nuclear responsibles and maintaining a system of nuclear non-proliferation did not appeal to a number of states outside the P5 that had little confidence in the UN security system, and preferred to rely on their own means of deterrence.[3]

Secondly, in some writings on international relations it is claimed that multipolar international systems are more war-prone than other types;[4] also that the international system since 1945 can be properly described as bipolar up to the end of the Cold War and unipolar thereafter. While both parts of this claim are open to contestation, it merits consideration as one possible level of explanation.

Thirdly, the decline in the number of international wars might be a long-term consequence of a widespread reaction to the excesses of two world wars, and the determination not to repeat mistakes of the past. This determination led, among other things, to the development of regional international organisations – including the European Union, whose explicit purpose was to make another war in Europe unthinkable.[5]

Fourthly, some of the decline may be attributable to the trend for states to conduct war through proxies. States have on many occasions over the past 60 years given assistance to particular governmental or rebel factions in civil wars, liberation struggles and regional conflicts. Such more or less covert involvement in ostensibly local wars may be motivated, at least in part, by a concern to circumvent the UN Charter's prohibition of armed attacks on member states.

A further, related, point is that a great deal of political change in the past decades, especially from the 1980s onwards, has been achieved through non-violent methods, rather than through war, civil or international. Such methods are not confined to constitutional change. In particular, there has been a noteworthy increase in civil (i.e., non-violent) resistance to authoritarian regimes and empires. The revolutions in Eastern Europe that contributed to the end of the Cold War are prime examples of this phenomenon. By hastening the end of the Cold War, these movements drastically reduced the danger of major international war in the form of conflict between the superpowers. Other notable cases of civil resistance include the resistance to the Marcos regime in the Philippines in 1986, the action against the coup in the Soviet Union in August 1991, and the revolutions in Serbia, Georgia and Ukraine in the years after 2000.[6]

Granted the variety of possible explanations for any reduction of inter-state war, it would be unwise to rush to make ambitious claims for the positive effects of international institutions in general, the UN in particular, or the Security Council even more specifically. Though the UN does deserve some credit, much of this is owed to parts of the UN system other than the Council.

The UN Charter and the organisation it created are based on a multi-pronged approach to the elimination of war between states, with the emphasis on equal rights and self-determination of peoples, and on the importance of tackling economic, social, cultural and humanitarian problems. Against this background, the particular tasks assigned to the Security Council can be viewed as those of accident and emergency services. They are one part of the public-health systems of states, but are far from being the only, or even the most important, determinants of public health.

Nevertheless, the Council should be acknowledged for the role it has played in the reduction in the incidence and human costs of international war – a task that it was designed to tackle, on which it has been taking action of various kinds for over six decades, and in respect of which significant results can be shown. In addition, the demise of colonial wars owes something to the role played by the UN in assisting the process of decolonisation. Any achievements in this regard, however, are overshadowed by the prevalence of civil and international wars in many parts of the post-colonial world.

The problem of civil war and other forms of conflict

The problem of civil war, which increased fairly steadily from the 1950s and peaked in the early 1990s, persists, and terrorism has increased since the late 1960s. In many cases these phenomena can be viewed as consequences of European decolonisation – a process that resulted, all too often, in a transition that was felt to be incomplete, in new states that lacked legitimate institutions and borders. After 1989, the collapse of the two communist federations of Yugoslavia and the Soviet Union left similar problems.

Throughout the period since 1945, civil wars have been a principal preoccupation of the Security Council. In many cases, the problem has been compounded by the involvement of outside powers, often on both sides, creating the new and little-recognised category of 'internationalised' civil war, mentioned above. Successive wars in Afghanistan and Bosnia had an internationalised character, as did the war in South Vietnam in the 1960s and early 1970s.

Civil wars, whether or not internationalised, present particularly difficult problems for international bodies. In such wars, violence and terrorism can easily become endemic in society. Not only is there seldom a clear case of 'aggression', but also it is not obvious what is the status quo ante to be restored. Civil wars often have a 'winner takes all' character, making mediation and conciliation especially challenging. There are inherent hazards in treating governments and insurgents as equal parties in negotiations, yet refusal to do so may lead to the collapse of diplomatic efforts. In wars involving insurgents or non-state parties, some belligerents have shown no regard for the UN in general or Security Council actions in particular: UN forces and personnel have been attacked or kidnapped with alarming frequency. The hope that the Council's international legitimacy, and the strength of the powers represented on it, would engender near-automatic compliance with the mandates of peacekeeping forces has evaporated. As if these challenges were not enough, outside powers typically see particular civil wars in very different ways, and therefore have substantial trouble agreeing on a strong course of action. The bulk of these problems and more besides have been experienced by the UN Security Council throughout its existence.

Terrorism remained mostly unaddressed by the Security Council during the Cold War, despite a surge in international terrorist activity in the 1970s and a consequent increase in concern about the issue on the part of P5 members. Cold War divisions, and the association of much international terrorism with the contentious issue of the Middle East, made it difficult for Security Council members to reach agreement on action against terrorism. The problem of defining terrorism and the controversial application of the terrorism label to liberation movements in the developing world, for example the notorious designation by the US and the UK of the African National Congress in South Africa as a terrorist organisation in 1987–8, compounded the Council's difficulties in addressing the issue.[7]

Since the end of the Cold War, and in particular since the 11 September 2001 attacks, the Council has been increasingly active in addressing the threat of international terrorism, especially through sanctions on states suspected of sponsoring terrorism (for example Sudan, Libya and Afghanistan[8]) and the establishment of mechanisms to curtail terrorist financing.[9] In 2001, the Council set up a Counter-Terrorism Committee to monitor and assist the counter-terrorism efforts of member states.[10] The Council has also come close to offering a definition of terrorism.[11]

However, there are clear limitations on the Council's ability to address the problem. Concerned about outside interference in and monitoring of their activities, states – the P5 in particular – have often been unwilling to internationalise their counter-terrorism efforts. The Counter-Terrorism Committee does not have any enforcement mechanisms that the Council could use to encourage compliance with its rules. Council members may disagree on what the causes of a particular form of terrorism might be, which can inhibit the Council's ability to identify clearly and address the problems and grievances that underlie terrorist acts. Finally, its lack of an intelligence capacity means that the Council may at times have difficulty establishing an accurate collective view of the origins of a particular terrorist attack. This was the case with the 2004 Madrid train bombings, which the Council hastily followed the Spanish government in attributing to the Basque separatist group ETA, though they were carried out by Islamist terrorists.[12]

The scope of Council action and inaction

By definition, the Council's selectivity involves both acts of commission and omission. Mostly it has been the latter, in particular the failure to address incidences of genocide and mass killings of civilians, that have undermined perceptions of the Council's legitimacy and effectiveness.

The limited role played by the Security Council in addressing crises and conflicts during the Cold War has generally been ascribed to the frequent use of the veto in the context of a polarising and all-encompassing superpower contest. However, while it is important, too much can be made of the veto. No veto prevented the Security Council from addressing the Khmer Rouge's auto-genocide in Cambodia between 1975 and 1979: the Soviet Union only vetoed a resolution in 1979 calling for an immediate ceasefire in the war with Vietnam and the withdrawal of Vietnamese troops.[13] At other times, Council members have acted in spite of a veto, for example over the Suez crisis in 1956, when the Council used the Uniting for Peace procedure to transfer the issue to the General Assembly, which then called for the establishment of the UNEF I peacekeeping operation.

Interventions by the superpowers within their spheres of influence – in particular in Latin America and Eastern Europe – were rarely even raised in the Council during the Cold War. In a notable exception, when the UK and France called on the Council to discuss the Soviet invasion of Hungary in 1956, they did so with the aim of distracting from their own activities in the Suez crisis. Revealingly, they failed to gain the support of the US, which lobbied intensively at the UN against any action over Hungary.[14]

One of the most troubling illustrations of the Council's selectivity, and its ineffectiveness in discharging its responsibilities for international peace and security during the Cold War, is the Iran–Iraq War, a conflict which began with an unambiguous Iraqi onslaught on Iran, and in which, during its eight-year duration, hundreds of thousands of people died, chemical weapons were used, and civilian areas and commercial shipping were routinely targeted. Especially in the early years of the war, the Council proved unable and unwilling to act, other than to issue statements expressing the hope that the belligerents would desist. Indeed, P5 states spent much of the war supplying arms, materiel, dual-use items and financial credits to one or other of the belligerents, and sometimes to both, helping the war efforts of both countries. Furthermore, the statements of the Council itself generally portrayed both parties to the conflict as being involved in violations of the laws of war, such as the use of chemical weapons, whereas in fact Iraq was the main offender in such matters. The Council failed to act more fairly and decisively on the Iran–Iraq War not because of any threat or use of the veto, but because four of the five permanent Council members were hostile to Iran. [15]

It took 11 years for the United Nations to determine that Iran had been a victim of aggression by Iraq in 1980. In December 1991, UN Secretary-General Javier Pérez de Cuéllar issued a report to the Security Council stating that Iraq had been responsible for starting the Iran–Iraq War:

> It is evident that the war between Iran and Iraq, which was going to be waged for so many years, was started in contravention of international law, and violations of international law give rise to responsibility for the conflict ... [16]

The fact that it took the UN so long to take serious account of the fact that Iraq had engaged in aggression must today make Iran – and many other states – nervous about leaving its security to any international organisation. The case of Iran confirms that even if a state is a member of an institution claiming to uphold, at the very least, certain elements of a collective security system, other states may prove to be unwilling to defend that state when it comes under assault.

Since the end of the Cold War, Council activity has markedly increased, and has assumed a wide variety of forms, some of which have been innovative. In the early 1990s, the Council took wide-ranging action in the

Balkans, Haiti and Somalia – including sanctions, peacekeeping, humanitarian intervention and the use of force to restore a democratic government. However, the problem of Council inaction in certain crises continued. The Council showed great reluctance to engage with the brutal conflicts in Liberia, Sierra Leone and the DRC, as well as with the genocide in Rwanda. The contrast between the Council's responses to the different crises of this period cannot be explained by the veto. Rather, it reflects the conscious collective choices of Council members. In light of the Security Council's apparent lack of interest in certain African conflicts in the early 1990s, it is unsurprising that the Constitutive Act of the African Union specifies that the African Union Assembly has the right to intervene in a member state 'in respect of grave circumstances, namely: war crimes, genocide and crimes against humanity', with no mention of any requirement for Security Council authorisation.[17]

The relatively feeble action of the Council on the humanitarian emergency that developed in Darfur from 2003 onwards has often been attributed to the threat of a veto from China, keen to protect its economic interests in Sudan. However, despite Western states' rhetoric about genocide and their calls for stronger action, these states' desire to involve themselves more deeply in the conflict through a robust peacekeeping operation or a non-consensual humanitarian intervention has clearly been limited. The anticipated Chinese veto, and calls from African states on the Council for work towards a solution through African institutions, may well have provided convenient excuses for avoiding more forceful action.

Unintended effects of ceasefire demands, peace agreements and peacekeeping operations

Sometimes the UN, including the Security Council, may affect the conduct of war in unanticipated and paradoxical ways. The possible role of the Charter's prohibition on armed attacks on member states in motivating indirect involvement in civil wars is an example of such unintended consequences. In addition, specific Council actions and modi operandi may also produce unanticipated responses.

Ceasefire demands and blitzkrieg strategies

Demands for ceasefires, so often made by the Council in response to new or ongoing hostilities, can sometimes accentuate the tendency for one or both parties to engage in blitzkrieg tactics. There is ample evidence from wars in the UN era – especially those between Israel and its Arab neighbours, and between India and Pakistan – that concern about impending

UN Security Council and General Assembly ceasefire resolutions has led armed forces and governments to rush to achieve their objectives quickly, before the pressure for a ceasefire (especially if supported by the US) becomes irresistible.[18]

Peace agreements followed by resurgence of violence
An even more worrying effect can flow from certain peace agreements: it appears that attempts at peacemaking can on occasion trigger renewed conflict. In the post-Cold War period, there have been at least three major examples of UN-brokered peace agreements that were intended to end civil wars, but which were followed by campaigns of extreme violence:

- The 1991 Bicesse Accords for Angola. These provided for troop demobilisation and multi-party elections. However, the rebel UNITA movement refused to accept the results of elections held the following year, and Angola returned to bitter civil war.
- The 1993 Arusha Accords for Rwanda. These provided for a nego-tiated end to the war between the Rwandan government and the Rwandan Patriotic Front, including through the establishment of joint transitional institutions. Following a number of incidents after the accords were signed, extremist elements in the government launched a campaign of extermination of the Tutsi population of Rwanda.
- The 1999 Lomé peace agreement on Sierra Leone. This offered immunity to forces which had systematically raped and mutilated thousands of fellow citizens.[19] The agreement and ensuing deploy-ment of peacekeepers were followed by further fighting, and the situation only stabilised following a UK military intervention in May and June 2000.

Peace agreements, especially if pressed on reluctant parties by outside bodies, can lead to an upsurge in conflict. This is partly because peace-making and conflict prevention necessarily require at least some of those involved in a dispute to modify their political demands, to forego the spoils of war, to abandon their dreams, or to make peace with those they dislike and distrust. Parties to conflicts often find it difficult and painful to do these things. None of this suggests that the UN should abandon the pursuit of peace agreements. However, it does underline the importance of exercising judgement about whether, when and how a peace agreement should be pursued, assessing above all the willingness of the parties to end a war in which they have been engaged.

Problems with peacekeeping under non-UN command

An indirect unintended effect of UN actions relates to certain peace-keeping operations led by regional institutions. The UN has done much to inculcate a norm of peacekeeping, and it is a tribute of sorts to the UN that the post-Cold War period has seen a considerable expansion in the number of non-UN military forces with peacekeeping and observer functions. Many of these forces, although not under direct UN control, are authorised or endorsed by the Security Council. However, some have not been authorised or endorsed by the Council, and, at times, parties to conflicts have seen some forces of this type not as peacekeepers, but as themselves interested parties to a conflict. An example can be found in the Russian-led CIS peacekeeping force deployed in the Georgian breakaway republic of Abkhazia following the 1993 and 1994 ceasefire agreements between Georgia and the Abkhaz authorities. In Georgia, the presence of Russian forces on Georgian territory was widely seen to represent a threat to the country's territorial integrity;[20] and in 1996, an account of the CIS deployment suggested that the force had violated all the key principles of peacekeeping, including impartiality, deployment on the basis of host consent and the use of force only as a last resort.[21]

Three main categories of Council-mandated and endorsed operations

The creation, mandate-setting and winding-up of UN forces and missions, including the authorisation of action by coalitions of states, is a major responsibility of the Security Council. Terms such as 'UN force' and 'UN mission' are often used loosely. In actual practice, there have been three very broad categories of forces and institutions operating with some degree of Council authorisation, recognition or supervision. There is some overlap between the categories.

UN peacekeeping operations

This type of operation consists of forces under UN command and control whose purpose is to observe and facilitate implementation of a cease-fire or peace agreement. Peacekeeping operations have been used in both international and internal conflicts. Deployed with the consent of the host state(s) and committed to impartiality, peacekeeping operations have generally helped to mitigate the conflicts into which they have been sent; during the Cold War, they also managed to an extent to isolate these conflicts from the East–West conflict, their presence helping to obviate the need for any direct involvement of (and thus confrontation between) the superpowers.

Almost all UN peacekeeping operations have been set up and managed by the Security Council: only in a few exceptional cases has the General Assembly taken on this role. The military component of a peacekeeping operation normally consists of a number of lightly armed national contingents deployed in a force under UN command. While they do not have combat functions, peacekeeping operations have a right to use force in self-defence and, depending on their mandate, for certain other specified purposes.

The distinction between peacekeeping and the enforcement of a peace agreement or ceasefire, although clear in principle, has sometimes been less clear in practice, and UN peacekeeping forces may become involved in, or associated with, enforcement. Several peacekeeping operations have had prominent enforcement as well as peacekeeping roles. This has been increasingly the case since the Cold War, a trend discussed in more detail below. The mandates of such forces have recognised the need for coercive action in various ways, sometimes by adding new mandates to earlier ones that had been based on more consensual assumptions. Examples of UN peacekeeping forces that had authorisation to engage in extensive coercive activities and which did so in at least some phases of their operations include ONUC in the Congo from 1960 to 1964, UNPROFOR in the former Yugoslavia from 1992 to 1995, UNOSOM II in Somalia from 1993 to 1995 and UNAMSIL in Sierra Leone from 1999 to 2005. Except for ONUC, all of these peacekeeping forces had, on paper, a strong mandate to use force, each making explicit mention of Chapter VII of the Charter, but all experienced major problems in carrying out the combination of peacekeeping and use of force.

In some cases, as in Bosnia from 1992 to 1995, Somalia from 1992 to 1993 and Rwanda in 1994, UN peacekeeping forces have operated in conjunction with UN-authorised forces that have enforcement functions and are under the command and control of a state or alliance (in these cases, NATO, the US and France respectively).

Finally, in a few cases, there has been a degree of cooperation between a UN peacekeeping force and a national force which, without formal Security Council backing, has assisted the peacekeeping force in carrying out some of the Council's objectives. In Namibia in 1989, for example, UN representatives on the spot tacitly acquiesced in a South African use of force to stop the infiltration of members of the South West Africa People's Organisation into Namibia in violation of ceasefire terms, assisting the work of the UNTAG peacekeeping force; and in Sierra Leone in May 2000, there was effective cooperation between UNAMSIL and a UK joint task force.[22]

UN institutions, missions and forces not classified as peacekeeping operations

In addition to peacekeeping forces, many other types of UN and UN-authorised body have operated in the field, working to manage and resolve conflict and address its consequences. These bodies, which may be authorised by a variety of UN organs, including the Security Council, the General Assembly and the Secretary-General, have taken a very wide range of forms, reflecting the broad scope of the UN's response to the problem of conflict.

At one end of the force/consent spectrum, any operation that was firmly under UN control and had enforcement functions, but was not classified as a peacekeeping operation, would belong in this category.[23] At the other end, the category encompasses the good offices missions set up by the Secretary-General for mediation in conflicts.

Several of the UN's numerous operations and institutions for tackling conflict were established by the Security Council. These include judicial and investigatory institutions, such as tribunals, for example the international criminal tribunals for the former Yugoslavia, set up in 1993, and Rwanda, set up in 1994; and investigatory panels and missions, such as the Mehlis inquiry, appointed in April 2005 to investigate the assassination of the former prime minister of Lebanon, Rafik Hariri. The Council has also been responsible for missions to aid the implementation of peace agreements – for example, the UN Assistance Mission in East Timor, set up in June 1999, and the UN Mission in Côte d'Ivoire, set up in May 2003. Missions have been established to deal with particular aspects of the aftermath of conflict, for instance to monitor disarmament – UNSCOM and UNMOVIC in Iraq are examples of this kind of operation. Also among the arrangements initiated by the Security Council have been missions to provide humanitarian assistance and help with post-conflict reconstruction following the defeat of an incumbent government, such as the UN Assistance Mission in Afghanistan, set up in March 2002, and the UN Assistance Mission for Iraq, which was established by a Security Council resolution of 14 August 2003, but whose activities were curtailed by the bombing of the UN's Baghdad headquarters on 19 August 2003.

Many UN forces and missions with significant roles in the security field were set up and managed by bodies other than the Council. Some were established by the Secretary-General, and merely noted by the Council, such as the investigation into allegations of the use of chemical weapons in the Iran–Iraq War, which operated from 1984–8, and election-monitoring and civilian-support missions in which there was no peacekeeping element, such as the UN Observer Group for the Verification of Elections in Nicaragua

Table 2: UN-authorised military operations, 1945–2007

Years	Lead country or international organisation									
	Australia	AU	ECOWAS	EU	France	Gabon[1]	Italy	NATO	UK	US
1946–1955										Korea (1950–3)
1956–1965										
1966–1975									Naval patrol (Rhodesia, 1966–75)	
1976–1985										
1986–1995					Operation Turquoise (Rwanda, 1994)			Operation Sharp Guard (Adriatic Sea, 1992–6) Operation Deny Flight (Bosnia, 1993–5) IFOR (Bosnia, 1995–6)		Iraq naval blockade (1990–2003) Gulf War (1990–1) UNITAF (Somalia, 1992–3) MNF (Haiti, 1994–5)
1996–2005	INTERFET (East Timor, 1999–2000)	AMIS (Darfur, Sudan, 2004–7)	MICECI (Côte d'Ivoire, 2003–4) MNF (Liberia, 2003)	Operation Artemis (DRC, 2003) EUFOR/ Operation Althea (Bosnia, 2004–)	Operation Licorne (Côte d'Ivoire, 2003–)	MISAB (Central African Republic, 1997–8)	MPF (Albania, 1997)	SFOR (Bosnia, 1996–2004) KFOR (Kosovo, 1999–) ISAF (Afghanistan, 2002–)		MNF (Iraq, 2003–) MIF (Haiti, 2004)
2006–2007		AMISOM (Somalia, 2007–)		EUFOR RD Congo (DRC, 2006) EUFOR TCHAD/RCA (Chad/ Central African Republic, 2008–)						
TOTAL	1	2	2	4	2	1	1	6	1	7

1 The MISAB mission led by Gabon involved troops from five other African countries, as well as French logistical support. Gabon's leadership of the mission was primarily political, rather than military.

from 1989–90, and the UN Guards Contingent in Iraq in May 1991, set up following the establishment of 'safe havens' in northern Iraq to enable Kurdish refugees to return home. Others were created by the General Assembly, such as certain missions concerned primarily with human rights and related issues, e.g., MINUGUA in Guatemala, established in 1994, which was tasked with verification of the implementation of ceasefire terms, human-rights monitoring and institution-building before and for some time after it was briefly given a peacekeeping mandate from January to May 1997.

UN-authorised military operations

This third type of operation consists of forces that have a specific mandate from the Security Council, but are not under direct UN control. They are typically under the command and control of a member state, or a group of member states – for example, an alliance or a regional organisation – and are generally referred to as 'UN-authorised forces', rather than 'UN forces', wearing national uniforms, not blue berets/helmets.

While non-UN military operations authorised by the Security Council can have purely and narrowly peacekeeping functions, generally such forces have had specific authority to use force for purposes that go beyond self-defence. There have been 27 explicit Security Council authorisations to states or alliances to command and control particular operations in which there was authority to use force. These cases are listed in detail in the Appendix, along with a short preface listing other types of case in which the Security Council indicated a degree of approval of actual or projected uses of force. The 27 explicit authorisations are also shown in Table 2, which demonstrates the range of countries, international organisations and alliances entrusted with leadership of such operations.

The functions of these authorised military operations have been varied, and have included the following:

- coercion in support of UN-mandated measures such as sanctions (the US-led naval forces in the Persian Gulf between 1990 and 2003 and NATO naval forces in the Adriatic Sea from 1992 to 1996 were deployed to enforce sanctions against Iraq and some successor states to the Socialist Federal Republic of Yugoslavia, respectively);
- full-scale military enforcement to compel an adversary to reverse an act of aggression (for example the US-led actions against North Korea from 1950 to 1953 and Iraq in 1991);
- forceful intervention in a state for humanitarian purposes or to restore a democratically elected government (the US-led Unified

Task Force in Somalia from 1992 to 1993 and the French-led *Operation Turquoise* in Rwanda in 1994 are examples of the former, the US-led Multinational Force in Haiti from 1994 to 1995 the latter);

- implementation, involving enforcement, of a peace settlement (the NATO-led IFOR and SFOR in Bosnia from 1995 to 2004, EUFOR in Bosnia since 2004, and KFOR in Kosovo from 1999 all had this purpose).

Resolutions authorising enforcement operations make specific reference to Chapter VII of the UN Charter. As a result, these operations are often called 'Chapter VII operations'. However, this term can be misleading because resolutions concerning certain other types of operation, especially sanctions but also sometimes peacekeeping, have also been adopted under Chapter VII.

While the approach of authorising a state or an organisation to assume the leadership of a military operation has well tested merits, it has two serious defects. First, there is inevitably a perception that the leaders of a military operation are willing to act only because of particular interests, as distinct from the general good. Hence, for example, the regular accusations that the US was interested in military action against Iraq in 1991 and 2003, not because of concern to stop aggression or enforce disarmament, but to get its hands on oil. Hence, too, the criticism of the US when it is unwilling in particular crises to put its troops in harm's way despite the Security Council being in principle in favour of action – as in Rwanda in 1994. The second, related, defect is that differences can emerge between members of the Security Council and the state or other body leading a coalition about the continuation and interpretation of an earlier mandate to use force. This problem arose in the Korean War in 1950–3, and was also at the centre of a major controversy over Iraq in the first three months of 2003. The US claimed that earlier Council resolutions provided a basis for a continuing US right to use force to implement the 1991 ceasefire terms in relation to Iraq, while other states viewed it as essential to go to the Council again to seek specific authorisation for taking the major step of invading the country and deposing its government. The UK equivocated between these two positions. The tension between the body doing the authorising and the states working at the sharp end is an unresolved problem at the heart of the now-familiar UN practice of using authorised coalitions to enforce resolutions. This tension is probably unavoidable in a decentralised and necessarily politicised system of selective security.

CHAPTER THREE

Proposals for UN Standing Forces: A Record of Failure

Since the formation of the United Nations, the creation of a standing UN military force has repeatedly been proposed.[1] Such a force has been seen as a means of improving the organisation's response to urgent problems of international war, civil war and mass killings; as a way of expediting the provision of peacekeeping forces to back up ceasefire and peace agreements; and as a basis for preventive deployments to ward off imminent dangers. The Security Council has generally been envisaged as having a key role in the creation and direction of such a force.

The Charter basis

Chapter VII of the Charter provides for armed forces to be at the disposal of the Security Council exclusively in the context of enforcement operations. Yet despite much influential advocacy, these provisions have never been implemented.

In Article 43, all member states 'undertake to make available to the Security Council, on its call and in accordance with a special agreement or agreements, armed forces, assistance and facilities, including rights of passage, necessary for the purpose of maintaining international peace and security'. These agreements are supposed to be concluded 'as soon as possible on the initiative of the Security Council'. Article 44 provides that when the Council has decided to use force, states asked to provide armed forces for such operations may participate in the decisions of the Council concerning how their armed forces are to be employed. Article 45, written before the analyses of strategic bombing in the Second World War aroused serious doubts about the efficacy of air power, conjures up a vision of the UN's military role that has never come into effect:

> In order to enable the United Nations to take urgent military measures, Members shall hold immediately available national air-force contingents for combined international enforcement action. The strength and degree of readiness of these contingents and plans for their combined action shall be determined, within the limits laid down in the special agreement or agreements referred to in Article 43, by the Security Council with the assistance of the Military Staff Committee.

Articles 46–7 provide for the creation of the Military Staff Committee, to be made up of the senior military representatives of the P5. This committee was intended to 'be responsible under the Security Council for the strategic direction of any armed forces placed at the disposal of the Security Council'. Apart from the fact that the provisions for it confirm the special role of the P5 in the Charter conception, the Military Staff Committee has had little significance. When it was established, in 1946–7, it was asked to examine the question of contributions of armed forces to the Security Council. The committee duly published a report in which the five powers agreed, at least in theory, on the desirability of making forces permanently available to the Security Council.[2] However, the report reflected significant disagreements among the P5 about the size, composition and basing arrangements of national contributions. The whole enterprise was abandoned. This was part of a broader failure to implement the ambitious provisions of Chapter VII, which specified a framework for the maintenance and application of armed forces (including those of individual member states) under Security Council auspices. The major military powers have never used the Military Staff Committee to make joint plans for the application of armed force. The Committee's role could possibly have grown as Council practices developed in the post-Cold War era, especially as UN and UN-authorised forces lack clear common operating arrangements. However, this has not happened. This confirms that the idea of the UN itself being a significant military player remains as moribund today as it was in the Cold War.

Articles 48–50 of the Charter outline the involvement of states in carrying out measures decided upon by the Security Council. The Article 48(1) specification that some actions may be taken by groups of states rather than the membership as a whole shows that – in spite of the unambiguous provisions for standing forces elsewhere in Chapter VII – from the start, not all the UN's eggs were in the basket of collective security.

Proposals from Trygve Lie onwards

Trygve Lie, the first Secretary-General of the UN, was anxious to salvage something from the plans to have a permanent UN force directed by a properly functioning Military Staff Committee. He dealt daily with difficult situations, such as in Palestine, in which, in his judgement, the UN needed greater capacity to impose its will. This was among his reasons for pushing for standing forces – albeit ones with modest capacities and objectives. As he wrote in his memoirs:

> During the spring of 1948, when it was already evident that there would be no possibility of implementing Article 43 in the foreseeable future, I cast about with my advisers for a new approach that might provide the Security Council with some sort of armed force. The outbreak of hostilities in Palestine gave urgency to such thinking, and after much consideration I decided on at least floating a trial balloon for the idea of a small internationally recruited force which could be placed by the Secretary-General at the disposal of the Security Council.[3]

Lie's proposal for an armed force at the disposal of the Security Council ran into a barrage of difficulties. He progressively watered it down, first to a 'guard force', then to a 'UN Guard', and eventually to an emasculated 300-strong 'UN Field Service'. Available records show the nervousness of many states – not only the Soviet Union and its allies, but others, including the US, the UK and France – about the UN Guard proposal. The US stated: 'We are inclined to think that the [UN Guard] proposal was somewhat too ambitious, and that it did encroach somewhat on the military theme.'[4]

The pattern of initial bold proposal followed by retreat was re-enacted many times in the UN's history. Lie himself repeated it after the outbreak of the Korean War in 1950. He proposed a 'UN Legion', to be primarily composed of more than 50,000 projected volunteers for UN military service. Once again, the title of the proposed force had to be changed, this time to the anodyne 'UN Volunteer Reserve'. Having made the change, Lie subsequently concluded in a report in 1952 that the plan 'was administratively, financially and militarily impractical at the present time'.[5]

In 1957, US foreign policy think tank the Carnegie Endowment for International Peace produced a book advocating the creation of a UN force.[6] The following year, two leading American international lawyers crafted an ambitious scheme for a 'UN peace force', to consist of volunteers in a Standing Force of between 200,000 and 600,000 persons, plus a Peace Force Reserve of between 600,000 and 1.2 million: as far as the projected size of a UN standing force is concerned, this plan was the high-water mark.[7]

Between 1992 and 1995, there were more proposals and developments relating to standing forces under UN control than at any time before or since. These were partly, like *An Agenda for Peace*, products of the optimism of 1992. The waning and ending of the Cold War in the years 1986–91, the active role of the UN in addressing regional conflicts at that time and the decline in the use of the Security Council veto had all led to heightened expectations of what the UN could achieve. But the new focus on standing forces was also the product of sober appreciation of the limitations of the UN in addressing certain crises – especially, towards the end of the period, Rwanda.

No standing force was actually created as a result of any of these proposals. States were clearly nervous about making their forces available to the UN; about the possibility that the Security Council might be able to use force with a relatively free hand; and perhaps also about the risk that a UN force could be swamped by the sheer number of difficult and danger-ous tasks it might be asked to tackle.

The art of the possible

Actual practice has produced a rich variety of partial solutions to the problem of needing forces available to implement certain aims of the UN Security Council. In light of this fact, the failure to implement the many proposals for standing UN forces should not be seen as a complete abandonment of efforts to develop collective uses of armed force. On the contrary, the UN era has seen many variations on the collective security theme, including UN authorisations of the use of force under the leadership of a single state or alliance; the establishment of international peacekeeping forces, under both UN and regional auspices; and, in particular, standby arrangements, both regional and global, regarding the availability of national forces for a variety of operations, including UN ones. As in the 1950s, so in the years after 1992, it has been the development of peacekeeping that has led to the greatest pressure to strengthen standby arrangements. In 1994, a process began whereby existing UN standby arrangements for peacekeeping forces were gradually formalised into the UN Standby Arrangements System. But because states were anxious to retain control over the uses to which their forces were put, the revised arrangements specified states' control over the availability of national units.[8] The system was, and remains, limited in scope. It is explicitly based on conditional commitments from member states. Put differently, it represents a modest triumph for the selectivity of the member states.

CHAPTER FOUR

Innovation and Flexibility since the End of the Cold War

In operating in a manner which has differed in certain respects from the scheme envisaged in the UN Charter, the Security Council has often acted creatively. This tendency, which began during the Cold War years, has been particularly striking since the end of the Cold War. Among the Council's most important and controversial innovations to address the problem of war have been the expansion of the number and scope of peacekeeping operations, the administration of post-conflict territories for a transitional period, the expansion of the category of security threats, and attempts to secure compliance with the law of armed conflict. These innovations are discussed below. A further innovatory element has in turn affected each of these changes: the emergence of a multi-faceted and varied relationship between Security Council action and that of a number of key regional institutions.

The large quantity and varied character of the Council's post-Cold War activities has added new dimensions to the question of selectivity. The sheer amount of business with which the Council has been continuously confronted, particularly during the early 1990s, and the difficulty of meeting increased public expectations, has troubled both officials in the UN Secretariat and diplomats working on Council-related matters at the UN.[1] Indeed, the number of conflicts and crises that the UN has been expected to handle simultaneously has resulted in a UN version of the ancient problem of imperial overstretch. The Council itself, and UN member states more generally, have continuously been confronted with questions about which operations they should initiate and take part in; whether a given problem is best addressed by UN forces or by the forces of states and regional bodies; whether to view such challenges as international crime and climate change as proper parts of the Council's remit; and whether to assist in the arrest and trial of suspected war criminals.

Expansion of peacekeeping

The practice of peacekeeping has evolved significantly in the post-Cold War period. The number of peacekeeping operations has increased dramatically. During the 40 years from 1948 to 1987, only 13 operations were authorised by the Security Council and the General Assembly. In the following twenty years (1988–2007), the Council established a further 50.

Furthermore, the scope of the activities conducted by peacekeepers has widened significantly. While during the Cold War, the vast majority of operations supervised ceasefires and patrolled buffer zones (for example, UNEFs I and II in the Middle East and UNFICYP in Cyprus), the mandates of post-Cold War operations have been more wide-ranging and intrusive. In 1991, the ONUSAL peacekeeping operation in El Salvador was the first to include a human-rights division, and since then, almost all peacekeeping forces have had mandates to monitor and promote human rights.[2] Peacekeeping operations have been responsible for the organisation and monitoring of elections (e.g., UNTAC in Cambodia and MONUC in the DRC); have supported refugee return (e.g., UNPROFOR in Bosnia and UNAMIR in Rwanda); have implemented programmes to disarm and demobilise former combatants (e.g., UNAMSIL in Sierra Leone and UNTAES in Eastern Slavonia); have supported the delivery of humanitarian aid (e.g., UNPROFOR in the former Yugoslavia and UNOSOMs I and II in Somalia); and have been deployed to prevent the spillover into a country of a neighbouring conflict (UNPREDEP in Macedonia). Few developments, though, highlight the expanded scope of peacekeeping mandates as much as peacekeepers' involvement in the international administration of the post-conflict territories of Eastern Slavonia, Kosovo and East Timor, discussed below.

The mandates of peacekeeping operations have been increasingly 'robust', regularly involving 'Chapter VII powers', which enable the use of force in pursuit of an operation's mandate, as well as in self-defence. In addition, the role of host consent in determining whether an operation will go ahead has declined (with operations involving at times what can only be described as 'coerced consent'). Still, as Chinese support for the protracted resistance of the Sudanese government to the full deployment of the UN peacekeeping operation in Darfur indicated, consent remains important to many UN member states, especially in the developing world. Troop contributors are still often reluctant to supply forces for operations not based on full host-state consent.

Finally, the number of non-UN peacekeeping operations there have been since the end of the Cold War that have had specific authorisation or approval from the Security Council, but have not been not under the UN's immediate control, has been remarkable (these operations generally come within the category of UN-authorised military operations, outlined above in Chapter 2). Such operations have generally been regionally based. Examples include the NATO-led IFOR/SFOR and KFOR operations in Bosnia and Kosovo respectively, the ECOMOG operation led by ECOWAS in Liberia, and the African Union Mission that operated in Sudan from 2004 to 2007. The fact that the Security Council accepts that other organisations may perform such tasks, and that it has associated itself with some, but not all, regional operations with peacekeeping purposes, underlines the selective nature of the Council's engagement with wars.

International administration of post-conflict territories

In 1999, the Security Council established international administrations over two post-conflict territories, Kosovo and East Timor.[3] UNMIK and the UN Transitional Administration in East Timor (UNTAET) exercised supreme executive, legislative and judicial authority – including the power to sign international treaties.[4] These international administrations were established to govern the post-conflict territories for limited periods of time until disputes over the territories' status were resolved, or until their political and administrative institutions had been strengthened sufficiently to prevent the renewed outbreak of war.

There is no explicit Charter basis for the international administration of war-torn territories. Chapters XI and XII of the Charter contain articles dealing with the administration of various dependent territories, and include provisions for the UN trusteeship system. They apply to non-state territories and address the problem of decolonisation, not war. Article 78 of the Charter states explicitly that 'The trusteeship system shall not apply to territories which have become Members of the United Nations, relationship among which shall be based on respect for the principle of sovereign equality.'[5]

While there were limited attempts at international administration during the Cold War, as in the Congo in 1960–64 and in West New Guinea in 1962 (both dealing with the consequences of decolonisation), a comprehensive international administration, exercising full governmental authority, was not established until 1996, when UNTAES was set up to manage the integration of the Serb-controlled territories of Eastern Slavonia, Baranja and Western Sirmium into the state of Croatia over a period of two years.[6] Three years later, in June 1999, UNMIK was established to build institutions of self-government in Kosovo and work towards the resolution of the territory's status; in October 1999, UNTAET was mandated to prepare East Timor for self-government and independence.[7]

International administrations have remained a rare occurrence. While the Security Council has established a range of peacekeeping missions with state-building mandates similar to international administrations, these have generally not exercised the same comprehensive authority as the operations in East Timor or Kosovo. Instead, the Council seems to prefer the 'light footprint' approach, as advocated by UN diplomat Lakhdar Brahimi in relation to Afghanistan in 2001. While the post-Cold War international administrations have had some unquestionable successes, they have also been very costly, and are not seen as a viable option for addressing the consequences of conflict in large countries, such as the DRC or Somalia.

Expansion of the category of threats to international peace and security

Underlying many of the Security Council's innovations, in particular those that have come about since the end of the Cold War, has been an important normative shift that has manifested itself in the expansion of what the Council considers a threat to international peace and security.

The Charter's drafters, in deliberately refusing to specify particular acts or situations that would constitute such a threat, left the Council wide discretionary powers on when to take action, and where. Yet during the Cold War years, issues that fell under the domestic jurisdiction of states were generally regarded to be beyond the authority of the Council. Similarly, human-rights violations and humanitarian emergencies were not considered threats to international peace and security. Thus in December 1971, when India tried to justify its intervention in East Pakistan (now Bangladesh) to the Security Council on humanitarian grounds, highlighting violations by the Pakistani military regime of the human rights of the Bengali population, which were resulting in massive refugee flows to India, it failed to gain support from Council members other than the USSR and Poland.[8]

Since the end of the Cold War, there has been a substantial shift towards a deeper understanding of security.[9] The International Commission on

Intervention and State Sovereignty, an independent international body established by the Canadian government to report on such issues to the UN, reflected the human-rights aspect of this shift in its December 2001 report by invoking the idea of a 'responsibility to protect'.[10] The Council increasingly considers internal conflicts to be threats to international order. Almost all of the peacekeeping operations created since the end of the Cold War have been deployed in civil wars, rather than inter-state conflicts (the UN operation to end the war between Ethiopia and Eritrea in 2000, UNMEE, is a rare exception). The Council has authorised several humanitarian interventions, most notably in Somalia, Rwanda and Haiti.[11] Following the 11 September 2001 attacks, it has further involved itself in the domestic realm of states through its counter-terrorism 'legislation', in particular on measures that states should take to suppress terrorist financing.[12] The Council has also increasingly interpreted development and climate change as security issues, in ways that have drawn opposition from non-permanent members, highlighted by the acrimonious debates about the Peacebuilding Commission at the 2005 World Summit and the opposition of the G77 to the Council's session on climate change in April 2007.[13]

Seeking application of the law of armed conflict

Since the Six-Day War in 1967, the Security Council has involved itself with maintaining the laws of armed conflict, first reluctantly, then with greater intensity after the end of the Cold War.[14] More than 400 resolutions passed between 1993 and 2006 make reference to the law of armed conflict.[15] These resolutions have clarified the content and application of existing law, rather than changing it or creating new law.

Predominantly, the Council has concerned itself with the application of the law, though it has also helped to bring long-standing issues relating to the laws of war, including sexual violence in conflict, into public debate. Its resolutions have regularly highlighted violations of the law of armed conflict in wars and crises, and, in four resolutions passed since the middle of 1999 on civilians in armed conflict, the Council explicitly underlined its commitment to human security and the protection of civilians in times of war.[16] The Council has requested that the Secretary-General investigate specific alleged violations, and make recommendations as to how civilians in armed conflicts may be protected more effectively. To respond to such violations, it has mandated peacekeeping operations to monitor compliance with the law of armed conflict, and to establish institutions and initiatives to promote respect for the law, for example truth commissions and education and publicity campaigns. At times, the Council has imposed sanctions on countries for the violation of the laws of armed conflict, such as on Sudan and the DRC, both in 2005.[17]

Most significant has been the Council's role in establishing international criminal tribunals to deal with allegations of serious crimes committed during the conflicts in the former Yugoslavia, Rwanda, Cambodia, Sierra Leone and Lebanon.[18] These tribunals do not all have the same form. The Yugoslav and Rwandan tribunals are true international criminal tribunals, established by the Council using its Chapter VII powers to decide on measures to maintain or restore international peace and security. No state can refuse to recognise these tribunals, and the use of the Council's powers gives them as much legitimacy as the international legal system can muster. The other, later, tribunals were not set up by Security Council fiat, but through negotiation between the UN and the parties.[19] These hybrid national–international tribunals may apply equally high standards of justice, and be equally effective, though they appear to have faced greater challenges to their legitimacy. The move towards the negotiated model may signal a desire on the part of the Council to distance itself from the details of conflict management, leaving it with a role focused more on strategy and on support for efforts made by states directly involved.

Innovation and selectivity: two sides of a coin

This survey of variations on the Charter template is by no means exhaustive. A further important innovation has been the increased use of Security Council missions, sent to a conflict area to establish the facts of a conflict, to then work out the basis for a peace agreement, or publicise a situation and put pressure on the conflict parties to assent to a settlement.[20] Another is the evolving structure of committees for monitoring the implementation of sanctions. Increasingly, these committees may, for instance, be supported by committees of experts that conduct field research and observe the implementation and effects of sanctions on the ground, as for example in Liberia.[21]

The innovations described here highlight the flexibility of both the Charter and the Council's practice in its responses to the problem of war. They have been possible because of the discretionary powers that the Charter grants the Security Council: the UN's founders were acutely aware that international order is not static, and that the challenges to this order will evolve as well. The flexibility and innovation that the Council has shown in this regard is the other side of the coin of selectivity.

CHAPTER FIVE

Accountability and Reform

Ever since the creation of the UN in 1945, there have been repeated proposals for its reform, some of which have been implemented. There have also been growing demands for UN bodies, including the Security Council, to be subject to a fuller system of accountability. In addition, in response to some of the UN's perceived weaknesses, including ineffectiveness and selectivity in the face of threats to the peace, proposals for alternative institutions, such as a 'League of Democracies', have been put forward by academics and policymakers in the US.

Major proposals for changing the structure of the Security Council, and for introducing formal systems of accountability as a means of controlling its actions, have not been implemented, but some informal changes to how the Council operates have been introduced. While reform is a serious issue that will not go away, progress on it has been limited – in part because many proposals for change have been based on questionable assumptions about the nature of the UN and the causes of its troubles.

Security Council accountability

The widening scope of the Security Council's activity since the early 1990s has given increasing prominence to the question of its accountability.[1] Accountability is an elusive concept, especially when applied to international organisations.[2] In practice, as discussed below, accountability often boils down to the fact that governments and indeed publics keep an eye on the UN generally and the Council in particular, and will clip the UN's wings in one way or another if they do not agree with its policies. Thus the selectivity of the Security Council mirrors the selectivity of the member states.

Arguably, the budgetary power of the General Assembly creates some limited Council accountability. Under Charter Article 17, the Assembly has the power to 'consider and approve the budget of the Organization'. However, when the Security Council embarks on a costly new initiative such as setting up a peacekeeping operation, the costs are borne through special budgets over which the General Assembly has less control than it has over the regular budget. In respect of both the regular and special budgets, member states are obliged under the Charter to pay contributions assessed on percentage scales agreed by the General Assembly. Frequently in UN history, states have sought to exert pressure on either the Assembly or the Council – for example in response to the latter's establishment of a peacekeeping operation with which they disagree – by withholding parts of these dues.

Formalised accountability could perhaps come through 'review' of Council decisions by the ICJ. Judicial review of the Council was plainly not part of the founders' intention, and it is unclear whether the ICJ would, in a suitable set of circumstances, pronounce itself competent to enquire into the 'legality' of a Council decision. At present, review by the ICJ is a wholly hypothetical idea, devoid of political reality or any workable legal framework.

A negative assessment of certain formal ideas of accountability should not imply any dismissal in principle of the core notion that an organ such as the Security Council is accountable for its omissions as well as its actions, or that this accountability expresses itself in various observable ways. However, the Council's accountability is essentially political, and therefore unpredictable. Moreover, member states holding the Council to account is in practice hard to separate from the other numerous constraints that operate on the Council. Among the various elements of accountability and constraint at work is the degree of control the General Assembly exerts through the election of the Council's non-permanent members. But perhaps the most important control lies in the capacity of states to undermine Council resolutions through shoddy compliance and spurious implementation. The fact that states decide selectively whether they will provide contingents and resources for peacekeeping and other forces and bodies, and have at times illegally withheld payments due to the UN, constitute controls of a kind on the Council.

The Council has recognised the limits of its powers over states by being notably modest in its military demands. Although it is entitled under Chapter VII of the Charter to call on all states to join in a particular military action, it has never done so. Even in the extreme case of the Iraqi invasion, occupation and purported annexation of Kuwait in 1990, the Council confined itself to authorising 'Member States cooperating with the Government of Kuwait' to take military action.[3] This was an implicit recognition that not all states could be persuaded to take even a symbolic part in the military action.

In other crises there has been extensive evidence of the capacity of states to inhibit the UN in New York from taking even the most modest action in relation to peacekeeping forces. Marrack Goulding, former head of UN peacekeeping, has testified eloquently to how these factors are a continuous brake on UN action. They amount to a powerful – but worrying – system of control over the Council.[4]

Formal change: proposals for structural reform of the Security Council

The problems of accountability, the sometimes stifling effect of the veto and the failure of the Council to act in certain crises have led to frequent calls for reform of the composition and procedures of the Council. The demand for reform is also driven by the simple fact that there have been fundamental changes in the realities of power in the world since 1945, in particular the rise of major new powers, of which India and Japan are only the most obvious examples. If the Security Council were being formed afresh today, it would hardly be assigned the exact composition that it currently has. There are obvious dangers in having a Security Council that does not fully reflect today's power realities. Yet structural reform has proven elusive, and continues to face serious obstacles.

Three core reform issues have repeatedly emerged for discussion: the appropriate number of permanent and non-permanent members; the existence and scope of the veto power; and the number of votes required to pass resolutions. The main attempt at reform took place in 2005. Before that there were two other major initiatives: negotiations in 1963–5, which led to an increase in the number of non-permanent members from six to 10 (and with it an increase in the number of votes required to pass a resolution, from seven to nine); and negotiations from 1993 to 1997, which, while failing to achieve any substantial amendments to the composition of the Council to address the developing world's concern about its under-representation, did bring about important changes in the Council's procedures relating to the transparency of its deliberations and its communications with non-Council members (discussed in more detail below).[5]

In March 2005, ongoing debates on reform culminated in the recommendations of Secretary-General Kofi Annan to the member states in advance of the 60th anniversary meeting of the General Assembly in September that year.[6] Following the recommendations of the High-level Panel Report of December 2004, Annan presented member states with two reform options, under both of which the Security Council would increase in size from 15 to 24 members. Neither option involved any change to the number of veto-wielding powers – an aspect of the proposals that was contested by states seeking permanent membership.

Model A envisaged six new permanent members: two from Asia (where the leading candidates were India and Japan); two from Africa (where the main contenders were Nigeria, South Africa and Egypt); one from Europe (Germany); and one from the Americas (Brazil). In addition, there would be three new non-permanent members on a non-renewable two-year term.

Model B envisaged no new permanent members, but instead a new category of eight 'semi-permanent' members, elected on a regional basis for a renewable four-year term; plus one new non-permanent member on a non-renewable two-year term. Model B was fiercely opposed by those countries (particularly Japan and Germany) that had been lobbying for a number of years for a permanent seat. In the end, the negotiations over both models broke down, and the outcome document of the 2005 World Summit said little on Council reform.[7]

It is questionable whether the two proposed solutions were the right ones for the UN in the current context of global politics. Both models took a narrow view in their diagnosis of the problem, and their prescription for addressing it.

Firstly, the reform proposals and the surrounding debate appeared to assume that the weaknesses of the Council were due, not to the complexity of the problems it faces and the inherent limitations within which its members must operate to tackle them, but rather to the Council's composition and the veto. The Council's record over the past three decades does not necessarily support this assumption. The fact is that since the end of the Cold War the Council has been much more active in its management role, and the veto has been employed much less frequently. The breakdown of consensus over Iraq in 2002–3, which sparked the renewed calls for reform, was regrettable, but it is not clear that a larger Council would have been any more likely to agree on a particular course to address the crisis.

Secondly, as many observers have noted, the desire for inclusiveness needs to be balanced against the objective that preoccupied the UN's founders: to avoid replicating the mistakes of the League of Nations. While the General Assembly was to represent the views of the entire membership of international society, when it came to the design of the Security Council, the body primarily responsible for managing threats to peace and security, equal representation and consensus decision-making had to be balanced against the practical need for responsiveness and effectiveness.[8]

Thirdly, the proposed mechanism for enhanced representation regional groupings – raises a key question: would the new members actually represent their regions (and if so, through what mechanism?), or would they simply be from those regions? These are two very different propositions, and divisions within regions remain significant. It is noteworthy that some of the loudest opposition to aspiring candidates in 2005 was voiced by their neighbours (for example by Pakistan in the case of India's candidacy, and China in the case of Japan's). Moreover, without explicit means for consulting with other member states or non-governmental organisations, the addition of new members will not automatically enhance representativeness.

The 2005 reform proposals largely made representativeness, as signalled by more seats for the developing world, a proxy for legitimacy. But if the goal is greater legitimacy, then it could be argued that less attention needs to be paid to questions of size, and more to the tricky question of how to enhance the accountability and transparency of the Council.

It is sometimes said that greater representativeness would reduce the selectivity of the Council, and might help to prevent situations such as that regarding Rwanda in 1994, where intervention was not in the national interest of any of the major Security Council members, and the Council thus failed for a long time to address the genocide. However, the link between regional representation and Council activity in that region is not clear. While African states are under-represented on the Council, Africa has been a key Council concern over the last ten years, and ten of the 17 ongoing UN peacekeeping operations are located in Africa. It is also unclear whether greater African representation would lead to more forceful UN activity in the continent to address humanitarian emergencies and large-scale human-rights violations – to more peace enforcement, rather than merely consent-based peacekeeping. The fact that African Council members have generally taken a more conciliatory approach towards Khartoum on Darfur than have Western states suggests that it might not.

Finally, the reform proposals tabled in 2005 referred to the need for the Council to reflect 'the realities of power in today's world'. But it is not clear that these realities would translate into more permanent members. While states outside the P5 are clearly gaining in material resources and influence, the distribution of power in military terms has become much more uneven than it was 20 years ago – in favour of the US. As international relations analyst Edward Luck has argued, the real issue is not so much the Council's size, but rather the strained relationship that exists between the UN and the US. Any proposed changes must take this reality into account as well.[9]

Informal change: reforms to working methods

No Charter reform, and therefore no change in the Council's composition, can happen without the consent of each of the P5. As a result, a certain structural immobility is built into the very fabric of the UN, especially the Security Council. Although the failure of reform proposals over the decades has been often blamed on the P5 and their unwillingness to give up or share power, differences among regional groups of states and the broader UN membership have been no less important. The 'North–South divide' between developed and developing countries has made agreement on possible changes very difficult to achieve. This was particularly the case in 2005, with divisions manifesting themselves in bitter debates at the World Summit over the budget, the Peacebuilding Commission and the Human Rights Council.

However, while formal, structural change might be difficult to realise, the Council has changed some of its working methods to increase its effectiveness and address some of the criticisms about participation and accountability. When tackling conflicts and crises, in recent years the Council has frequently complemented its formal decision-making structures with informal, more flexible mechanisms – in particular, so-called 'informal groups' (contact groups and 'groups of friends'), which include non-Council member states that have a special stake or interest in a conflict. While the use of such informal groups goes back to the 1950s, their number increased dramatically in the 1990s, as the Council tried to adapt to the new realities of the post-Cold War world. Such groups allow greater flexibility and privacy, unconstrained by the procedures of formal Council meetings, as well as greater voice and involvement for important interested actors who are not Council members, such as key regional powers, major donors and countries trusted by the conflict parties. This involvement enables the mobilisation of extra diplomatic and other resources for conflict resolution.[10]

Since the early 1990s, there has been a range of other changes designed to increase transparency and participation in Council decision-making (the so-called 'Cluster II' reforms). These include:

- Fuller and quicker publication of Council draft resolutions and other documents, including its monthly programme;
- Increased involvement of troop-contributing countries in debates on the mandates of peacekeeping operations. Since 2001, the Council has held mandatory closed sessions with troop contributors before deciding on new mandates or mandate changes;[11]
- Greater dissemination of information about the work of sanctions committees and other subsidiary bodies to non-Council members, e.g., through regular briefings after meetings;
- Increased involvement of non-members in Council sessions.[12]

Most of these reforms came about as a result of pressure from the General Assembly or non-permanent members. The P5 have at times been resistant, but they have generally embraced and promoted particular reforms. However, while the changes are important, their impact should not be overstated. Troop-contributing countries, for example, regularly complain about the lack of opportunity for real input at the closed Council meetings, arguing that mandates are effectively written before they are consulted. Similarly, increased opportunities for the participation of non-Council members in Council sessions have been undermined by the growth of informal (and non-public) consultations between Council members, in which it appears that most decisions are taken. In the absence of agreement on structural reform of the Security Council at the 2005 World Summit, the outcome document called for further efforts to enhance transparency and wider participation in Council decision-making.[13]

Proposals for an international organisation of democracies
In the United States, perceptions of the UN as ineffective or politically compromised have contributed to the development of proposals for a 'concert' or 'league' of democracies. The assumption underlying such proposals is that the Council's failings are a consequence of the membership and veto power of non-democratic states. In 2006, the Princeton Project on National Security proposed a Charter for a Concert of Democracies. The new organisation was intended to complement the Security Council, but in the event that reform of the Council 'failed', it was to have the power to authorise the use of force via a two-thirds majority of its members, particularly in connection with a 'responsibility to protect' citizens against predatory or failing governments.[14] In the 2008 US presidential campaign, the theme of such an organisation was picked up by Republican presiden-

tial candidate John McCain, who proposed the establishment of a League of Democracies:

> We need to renew and revitalise our democratic solidarity. We need to strengthen our transatlantic alliance as the core of a new global compact – a League of Democracies – that can harness the great power of the more than 100 democratic nations around the world to advance our values and defend our shared interests.[15]

The response of the many potential members of this proposed league has been muted. This in itself confirms one central weakness of the proposal: democracies do not have the strong shared understanding of, or willingness to act regarding, a wide range of international issues that the concept assumes them to have. In addition, the theory behind these proposals – that the ineffectiveness and selectivity of the Council are primarily the result of the presence of non-democratic states – is deeply flawed. The UN's weaknesses have many other causes as well, including the diverging interests of its democratic members. An interpretation of the Security Council's failings that neglects the wide range of factors that have contributed to its troubles is a poor basis on which to propose an alternative or supplementary institution. In view of members' diverging interests, the exclusion of a strong decision-making hierarchy from the various proposals for a union of democracies is another potential source of weakness: it was with good reason that, in 1944–5, US negotiators insisted on a strong Security Council with special prerogatives for its permanent members. Finally, the proposals for a new league fail to recognise explicitly that a central task of international diplomacy is to deal with, and work out a modus vivendi among, the many different types of political system that exist in a plural world; and that democracy may be better advanced through a universal organisation than through a club of like-minded states.

Problems and Opportunities of Selective Security Today

This paper has suggested that the selectivity that characterises the actions of the UN Security Council, and the nature of the system over which it presides, has a number of distinct forms:

- Selectivity of the Council, and especially of the P5, in deciding which issues to address or not address.
- Selectivity of the Council in the framing of a problem and in determining which of a wide range of possible actions to take in respect of a particular crisis.
- Selectivity of all UN member states regarding their willingness to provide military and material resources for Council-mandated activities and operations.
- Selectivity of states involved in conflict about whether they wish the conflict to be referred to and addressed by the Council.
- Selectivity of all the above actors in the choice of whether to handle an issue through other organisations, regional or global – whether as a complement to, or a substitute for, the direct involvement of the UN Security Council.

Selectivity in all these forms affects everything the UN Security Council does, as well as how it is perceived. An exploration of the implications of this selectivity must start with an overall appraisal of the Council, the performance of which is the subject of sharply differing interpretations.

Some have seen the Council as a failure – and there is no denying that it has fallen short of the goals set for it in the Charter. Others have seen it primarily as a success – because of the diminution in inter-state war, for instance, and the Council's role in assisting great-power collaboration, however limited and flawed this may be. Yet it is possible to make a more fine-grained and evidence-based judgement than the classic 'glass half-empty' versus 'glass half-full' debate might suggest.

Our summary of the weaknesses and strengths in the Council's record is necessarily imperfect. It is not always easy to distinguish the effects of Council action and inaction from the role played by other factors in world politics, or indeed from the effects of other UN agencies, particularly the General Assembly. Moreover, aspects of the Council's record are deeply ambiguous and hard to categorise as either strengths or weaknesses.

Despite the ambiguities, it is clear that for many policymakers, the role of the Council remains pivotal. As the International Commission on Intervention and State Sovereignty put it in 2001: 'There is no better or more appropriate body than the United Nations Security Council to autho-rise military intervention for human protection purposes. The task is not to define alternatives to the Security Council as a source of authority, but to make the Council work better than it has.'[1] This view was echoed by both the High-level Panel in 2004 and the Secretary-General's reform propos-als of 2005. These statements reflect a desire to maintain the Council's status within international society, and to avoid any further erosion of the social capital it draws upon to encourage the cooperation of UN member states.[2]

Weaknesses in the Council's record

The Security Council's legitimacy and effectiveness in addressing the problem of war and authorising the use of force have been called into question on many occasions. The Council has been criticised both when it has acted, and when it has not. Major controversies about the Council's role have revolved round the following ten issues:

Inaction. This has been a persistent theme throughout the Council's history. The Council's relevance to international crises is undermined by the fact that there have been numerous occasions on which it has been unable to reach decisions about particular wars and threats of war, whether because of lack of interest among the major powers, the resistance of those involved in a conflict, or a threat or use of the veto. The inaction of the Council or of forces operating under it was particularly notable in various crises connected to the Cold War, as well as the Iran–Iraq War, the mass killings in Rwanda in 1994 and the massacre at Srebrenica in Bosnia in 1995.

A particularly disturbing aspect of UN inaction is seen in the fact that states that enjoy a close relationship with a veto-wielding member of the Council can escape criticism or action from the Council. The most highly publicised case is Israel, which has been regularly let off the hook by a US threat or use of the veto. Similarly, though not so frequently, China has used its power in the Council to protect regimes, such as those in Sudan and Myanmar, from UN-authorised action.

Intelligence failures. In many conflicts and crises it has been painfully evident that the UN lacks its own reliable intelligence capacity, with the result that it does not have an independent capability for responding quickly to fast-moving events, and is at risk of acting on unreliable information. While it may not be feasible for the UN to develop an independent capacity to collect secret intelligence, it does need to develop an effective system for sharing and evaluating intelligence in certain issue areas.[3]

Weak assessment of situations. Operating as it does with imperfect information at its disposal, the Council has on occasion approached conflicts in questionable ways: for instance, when it has maintained a neutral stance in circumstances in which there is substantial doubt that a neutral position is appropriate; or when it has shown unnecessary haste in making a judgement about a crisis, most strikingly in its resolution blaming ETA for the Madrid train bombing of 2004.

Difficulty in agreeing on military action. The Council is generally better at agreeing on ends than on means. Even when its directives have been openly flouted, its members have often differed sharply about follow-up action, including the use of force, and have in the end been unable to agree on it. In some cases, such disagreement on the Council may be positive. However, two serious consequences can flow from failure to agree on specific military action. Firstly, to the extent that indecision becomes a pattern, it risks creating a perception of the Council as an organisation whose bark is worse than its bite, or as one that stands by while terrible crimes are committed. Secondly, in cases where there has been an initial authorisation to use force but then there is disagreement on how this should be followed up, the net effect may be that uncontrollable leeway is handed to the authorisee. This was part of the problem regarding Iraq in 2003, when a key question raised was the extent to which pre-existing authorisations to states or coalitions continued when the Council was unable to agree on new ones.

Reliance on the lowest common denominator. There has been a tendency for the Council to focus on 'lowest common denominator' policies – that is, those on which agreement is easy to reach. Such policies often relate to crisis points and short-term problems, and do not tackle the underlying issues at stake in a given conflict. Thus, in many conflict situations, the Council has justifiably called for immediate ceasefires, arms embargoes and urgent humanitarian action, but has been less effective in agreeing policies and actions to address the issues that gave rise to the resort to arms.

Uneasy relations with the US. The relationship of the Council with its most powerful member, the US, has proved perennially difficult. At least since the time of the Korean War, there has been a strand of thought among member states and observers that views the Council as essentially dominated by the US, and therefore a mere instrument of power politics, rather than a cure for it. This view, which is so corrosive of the UN's legitimacy, has become more widespread in the post-Cold War era because of the increased significance of the role of the US, both in the Council and in interventions around the world. At the same time, within the US, there is frequent criticism of the UN, including complaints that the UN framework entangles the US in a complex and unsatisfactory decision-making system, and places disproportionate burdens on it. Since 1945, the US has tended to see itself, rightly or wrongly, as a major provider of security outside a UN framework, for example through its network of alliances: against this background, the obligations arising from Council membership are sometimes presented as unnecessary additions to an already heavy burden.

Violations of the Council's resolutions by its members. On some occasions Council members, including members of the P5, have violated the terms of a Council resolution for which they voted, possibly because they had come to see its provisions as ineffective or damaging. For example, during the arms embargo on the former Yugoslavia from 1991–5, the US and other states connived in the illicit acquisition of weapons by several governments affected by the embargo, including Bosnia and Croatia. Other violations, arguably more damaging in their effects, include various breaches of the sanctions on Iraq between 1991 and 2003: these included Council members trading with Iraq, and the toleration of large-scale smuggling between Iraq and neighbouring states. Some of these developments helped to precipitate the Iraq crisis of 2003.

Poor management of force. The UN has at times proved ineffective in managing the use of force. While the Council has not been directly involved in force management, this problem has primarily been a consequence of the poor quality of certain Council mandates. For example, during UNPROFOR's involvement in the former Yugoslavia, there was strong criticism from military specialists that the Council had set over-elaborate procedures and over-precise rules for the use of military force in protecting the 'safe areas', so that, for example, force could only be used under a 'dual-key' arrangement, and even then, only with smoking-gun evidence against those directly responsible for violations of ceasefire agreements and the protected areas. It could not be used more generally against the forces that had instigated such violations.

Corruption and weak control of operations. Actions initiated by the Council have in some instances been marred by corruption scandals, such as that connected with the Oil-for-Food Programme, which operated from 1995 to 2003 as part of the Council's sanctions regime against Iraq.[4] There have also been instances of corruption in connection with contracts to supply certain UN peacekeeping operations;[5] and of unethical sexual conduct by UN peacekeeping personnel.[6] These cases have raised the question of whether the Council's members have involved themselves sufficiently in the detailed framing and subsequent implementation of its policies.

'Dustbin' and 'punchbag' roles. The UN in general, and the Security Council in particular, continues to play the role of a convenient dustbin into which states can throw issues on which they do not have the will or capacity to act; it also functions as a punchbag for states to hit when other possible targets of their wrath are more difficult to attack. Both these roles reinforce the Council's other weaknesses.

Some of the weaknesses listed above played a part in the Council's deplorable handling of certain crises – including Arab–Israeli problems since 1947, Iraq's invasion of Iran in 1980, and the killings in Rwanda in 1994 and in Darfur since 2003. The fact that the Council's record suffers from some or all of these defects is widely accepted. There are strong criticisms of the UN's performance in the security field in many countries and traditions of thought: the idea that there is a monopoly of such criticism in the US is wide of the mark.

Yet even if there is truth in all the criticisms levelled at it, the Council is not necessarily a failure. When people assert that the Council has failed, it is worth enquiring by what standard they are judging it, and what precisely their judgement means. If the Council's performance is judged against a high standard – for example, if it is viewed as a means of replacing war with law, as a presumed alternative to national defence efforts, or as a provider of the ambitious collective security scheme that the UN Charter is widely perceived as representing – then it is obviously a failure. If, alternatively, it is judged according to the benchmark of whether it has contributed to the management of certain crises in international relations and to a modest degree of stability, then it is at least a partial success.

Strengths in the Council's record

One of the key strengths of the Security Council in international society lies in its role as a 'collective legitimiser' of the use of force by member states.[7] While collective legitimation is not the exclusive preserve of the UN – other inter-governmental organisations (particularly regional ones) can also play a legitimising role – the UN has been the main focus of states' multilateral efforts to win approval for their policies. In some cases, the Council's endorsement can make a direct material difference, by enabling those leading a military action to obtain troops and financial support from other member states. More commonly, however, the UN stamp of approval has more intangible benefits: it enhances both the lawfulness and the political acceptability of the proposed military campaign. The so-called Just War tradition, which invokes a series of precautionary principles to help to determine the justifiability of a use of force, gives prominent place to the notion of 'proper authority'.[8] In the present era, the UN Security Council is widely seen as constituting that 'proper authority'.[9] As a result, states have invested significant diplomatic capital in garnering Council authorisation for their actions. Indeed, as the astute UN observer Inis Claude argued as long ago as 1966, 'the value of acts of legitimisation by the United Nations has been established by the intense demand for them'.[10]

A large array of claims can be made for the effectiveness of the Security Council. The eight most important are:

It has assisted in the reduction of the incidence of international war. While it does not amount to the removal of the scourge of war at which the Charter aimed, the reduction in the number and human cost of inter-state wars over the past decades is significant. Many other events, institutions and processes have contributed to this outcome, but the role of the Council in it is not negligible.

It has effectively opposed major invasions aimed at taking over states. A classic issue that any international organisation in the security field must tackle is a major attack by one state upon another. The Council's prompt responses to certain attacks – on South Korea in 1950, on Kuwait in 1990 – reinforced the message, which also came from other quarters, that aggression does not pay. The fact that the Council failed to respond to certain other major attacks, such as Iraq's invasion of Iran in 1980, weakens this message but does not invalidate it.

It has usefully deployed peacekeeping forces. In many cases, UN peacekeepers have helped to stabilise a volatile situation; in particular, some operations have prevented local conflicts from becoming arenas for great-power confrontation. There is also evidence that in some cases, the deployment of peace operations to a territory has helped to prevent the recurrence of civil war.[11]

It has provided a framework for assisting major changes in international relations. Perhaps the two most important changes in the structure of international relations in the UN era have been decolonisation and the end of the Cold War. While both developments have multiple causes, the UN in general and the Security Council in particular can be seen as having assisted them, by providing a forum for discussion between states and a framework through which post-colonial and post-Soviet states could assert their independence and develop relations with other countries.

It has adapted to new developments. The Council's activities have expanded to take account of new developments in the sphere of international peace and security, particularly in international humanitarian law; international criminal law; international efforts to assist the emergence and consolidation of democratic practices in states; and international efforts to combat nuclear-weapons proliferation and global terrorism.

It has assisted in the diffusion of norms. The Council has played a key role in the articulation and diffusion of norms, both new and existing. One long-standing example is the principle of self-determination, which over time both permanent and non-permanent members induced the Council to promote in its resolutions. More recently, the Council's statements and actions have contributed to the development of ideas of human security and the 'responsibility to protect'.

It has provided governance and institution-building capacities to war-torn and failed states. The Council has gradually developed a capacity for providing interim governance and assisting the re-establishment of the functions of government, including democratic processes, in states that have undergone civil war or external domination. Four leading cases are Cambodia (1992–3), Kosovo (since 1999), East Timor (1999–2002) and Afghanistan (since 2001). In each of these cases, large numbers of refugees returned: in Afghanistan, there were more than four million returnees between 2002 and 2006.

It has assisted great-power cooperation. Engaging in continual interaction and negotiation, the Council has helped to maintain a degree of understanding and cooperation between the great powers both during and after the Cold War, securing agreement on basic norms and helping to settle certain regional conflicts, for example in Central America. Even when agreement has been elusive, the Council has provided a forum where major powers can signal their intentions and the 'red lines' beyond which they should not be pressed.

Many other claims could be made for the Council's uses. Several relate to undramatic but important activities, such as the deployment of missions to conflict zones to gather facts and sketch the basis for peace agreements. The Council has made good use of panels of experts to assess the implementation and impact of sanctions, for example in Liberia and the DRC. It appears to have learned from the ineffectiveness and shocking side-effects of some past applications of sanctions, and is moving towards better-targeted measures. As for the future, in an era in which it is sometimes argued that there is a need for the preventive use of force to ward off threats to international peace and security, the UN Security Council is the one body in the world that has the explicit and undisputed legal right to take preventive action against such threats.

Selective security: implications for UN member states
The various kinds of selectivity that were foreshadowed in the Charter have formed a continuous thread throughout the UN's history, and are inescapably linked to both the weaknesses and the strengths of the Council's record.

The conclusion that flows from this analysis, that the role of the UN Security Council is unavoidably selective, is not likely to be an occasion for celebration. 'Selective security' is hardly an inspiring slogan. Indeed, it represents an admission that older kinds of power politics still survive in the UN era, albeit often in new forms. The two systems, that of the UN and that of various forms of power politics, operate in parallel, neither entirely trumping the other.

A degree of selectivity in the action of the Security Council, and UN member states more generally, is important, perhaps even desirable. It may reduce the danger of UN over-commitment: indeed, the selectivity of the UN's member states may have saved the organisation from direct involvement in ill-thought-out uses of force, such as that in Iraq in March 2003. The Council's selectivity also helps it to maintain great-power cooperation, and helps to make UN membership compatible with the interests and perceptions of the member states. In short, a system of selective security may be far more workable than more ambitious schemes for collective security.

The Council's selectivity has enabled it to respond flexibly to the changing nature of war. The reduction of major inter-state war, while far from amounting to its elimination, is a notable achievement of the UN era, especially in view of the vast increase in the number of states. At the same time, the character of war in general has evolved over the past 60 years in ways the drafters of the Charter never envisaged, and which have made it impossible for the UN to be directly involved in addressing all armed conflict: the all-encompassing polarisation of the Cold War, the prominence of intra-state conflict and the rise of terrorism are all phenomena that a more rigid classic collective security system would have found difficult to manage.

While selectivity has merits, it also inescapably involves dangers: it has resulted in inaction in crises where action would have been the better course; it has been at the heart of acrimonious arguments about the UN's troubles; and perceptions of selectivity have undermined the UN's self-projection as an impartial body, damaging the organisation's institutional legitimacy.

The various reasons for the UN Security Council's selectivity need to be understood: simplified views lead to bitter debates and ill-considered policy prescriptions. The selectivity of the Security Council is often assumed to have an essentially simple character, and to be attributable to a single cause: for example, the dominance of the US, or the use of the veto to inhibit necessary action, or the refusal of certain non-democratic members to approve action that might cause tawdry dictators to lose sleep. Yet we have seen that it also has other causes, including, often, the lack of interest among member states – democratic and dictatorial alike – in taking military action in aid of a distant and debatable cause. Further, the states in the international system have genuinely different experiences of war, which naturally colour their attitudes to proposals to use force under UN or any other auspices.

For UN member states, the most obvious implication of the UN's selectivity is that the degree of security it provides is at best partial: states need to retain other security arrangements, including provisions not only for national defence, but also for security through regional bodies and alliances. This is hardly a new lesson: it was implicit in the UN Charter itself, and has been understood by states throughout the six decades of the UN's existence.

Recognition of the unavoidable nature of the UN Security Council's selectivity has a further implication: that in formulating their statements and policies, states should devote less energy to criticising the UN for failing to live up to the impossible ideal of a comprehensive system of collective security, and more on developing a businesslike working relationship with the organisation, in which both its strengths and weaknesses are acknowledged as a shared starting point.

This conclusion is relevant above all to the United States, which has historically oscillated between excessive hope for the UN and angry disenchantment with it, an attitude seen by many as betraying more than a touch of arrogance. A new US administration needs to abandon rhetoric suggesting that US involvement in the UN, and in activities undertaken under Security Council auspices, necessarily implies a surrender of national sovereignty, or, specifically, a surrender of the US's existing right to use force to defend its interests. The US needs to develop an approach to the UN that recognises the organisation's achievements and strengths, while not dismissing the many justified criticisms of it, or denying the inherent difficulties of combining a system of global security based on US power with the US's responsibilities as a member of the UN Security Council. Plans for a League of Democracies or similar, arising as they do from deeply flawed assumptions about the causes of the UN's limitations and the nature of international order, do not represent a solution to these difficulties.

The need for a more realistic approach to the UN and its unavoidable selectivity also extends to those proponents of UN reform who call for the enlargement of the Council to make it more representative. While there is a powerful case for enlargement, and the issue cannot be wished away, a major increase in the membership (in particular the permanent membership) is unlikely to be agreed by all the necessary states, and, if it were to be agreed, would be unlikely to reduce the selectivity of the Security Council in any case. It would be more productive to continue to focus on reform of the Council's procedures and working methods, to increase its transparency and allow for greater participation of non-member states in its deliberations, in particular troop contributors and countries in the immediate neighbourhood of a state in conflict.

The difficulty of reforming the composition of the Security Council is likely to further increase the importance of regional and other international organisations. The most dynamic changes affecting the work of the Security Council since the end of the Cold War have occurred, not in the notoriously challenging area of Charter reform, but in an area no less significant in terms of the changing arrangements of power in the world: the security roles assumed by regional and international organisations, in many cases in close collaboration with the Security Council. The development and broadening of these roles is partly a reaction to the inherent limits to what the Council can achieve. It does not solve all problems of selectivity, and may make some more complex, but it does potentially reduce the salience of the most common complaint about selectivity, that the threat and use of the veto in the Security Council prevents any action on certain problems. Where the Council fails, other bodies may be able to carve out a role.

The Security Council retains its significance as the pre-eminent international body with a global role in the field of international security, but the very universality of its potential roles necessarily results in selectivity in practice. There may be merit in open acknowledgement of the fact that the Security Council system is characterised by selectivity. A recognition of the significance and multifaceted character of selectivity could provide a basis for realistic and constructive international debate about the Council's roles in relation to armaments and war. It could also help in the ongoing process of determining which types of issues and activities are best handled within a UN framework, and which are best handled by states and regional bodies. The Council remains a keystone of the international security architecture, but it cannot and does not hold up the edifice all on its own.

UN Security Council-Authorised Military Operations, 1950–2007

The table below lists in chronological order those military operations undertaken between 1950 and 2007 (some of which are still ongoing) that were explicitly authorised by the Security Council, that had powers to use force under Chapter VII of the UN Charter, and that did not operate under UN command and control.[1] None of these missions is listed by the UN Secretariat as a UN peacekeeping operation, but a range of them operated concurrently with, or were succeeded by, UN peacekeeping operations, and some of them had peacekeeping functions in their own right.

Certain operations do not conform to the above criteria, and therefore are not included in this list:

UN peacekeeping operations. In many cases, the Security Council resolution authorising a peacekeeping operation grants explicit authority under Chapter VII to use force for a wide variety of specific purposes. Nevertheless, as operations under direct UN command and control, these are not included here.

Non-UN operations that were authorised or endorsed by the Security Council, but did not have clear authority under Chapter VII to use force (for example, the NATO mission *Task Force Fox*, which monitored the implementation of a peace agreement in the former Yugoslav Republic of Macedonia in 2001 and 2002).

Non-UN operations that were endorsed by the Security Council only after they had already begun operating on the authorisation of a regional body or a state (for example, the ECOWAS intervention in Liberia in 1990).

Operations that the Security Council has endorsed (for example through a resolution or presidential statement) but has not formally authorised. An example of this is the Australian-led deployment of troops and police to Timor Leste in May 2006 (*Operation Astute*), which was welcomed by a statement from the president of the Security Council on 25 May 2006, and retrospectively endorsed by UNSCR 1690 on 20 June 2006.

Operations that were authorised, welcomed or endorsed by the Security Council, but which were not deployed, such as the Multinational Force in Zaire, authorised by UNSCR 1080 of 15 November 1996.

The US-led intervention in Afghanistan following the attacks of 11 September 2001. This action was based on the Security Council's explicit recognition of the right of the US to self-defence under Art. 51 of the Charter in UNSCR 1368 of 12 September 2001, but not on a specific Council authorisation.

Name/description of operation	Location and duration	Authorising Security Council resolutions (UNSCRs)	Details	Strength
US-led military coalition in Korea	Korea (1950-3)	83 of 27 June 1950; 84 of 7 July 1950	The Security Council (in the absence of the Soviet Union, which was boycotting the Council at the time) authorised the military coalition to assist South Korea 'to repel the armed [North Korean] attack and restore international peace and security in the area'.	c. 750,000 (incl. 340,000 from South Korea)
UK naval action in connection with economic sanctions against Rhodesia	Rhodesia (1966-75)	221 of 9 Apr 1966	The Council called on the UK to use force to prevent the delivery of oil for Rhodesia to the port of Beira in Portuguese Mozambique. A British patrol had been in place in Beira for several months before it was explicitly authorised by the Council.	
US-led naval blockade of Iraq, following the Iraqi occupation of Kuwait	Iraq (1990-2003)	661 of 6 Aug 1990, 665 of 25 Aug 1990	The Council called on member states to monitor and control shipping in the Persian Gulf to enforce sanctions on Iraq.	
US-led Gulf War coalition	Iraq (1990-1)	678 of 29 Nov 1990	Military coalition in the Gulf tasked with ending the Iraqi occupation of Kuwait and restoring peace and security to the area.	c. 540,000
Operation Sharp Guard	Adriatic Sea (1992-6)	787 of 16 Nov 1992	NATO naval forces tasked with enforcing the arms embargo and economic sanctions on successor states to the Socialist Federal Republic of Yugoslavia.	
US-led Unified Task Force (UNITAF)	Somalia (1992-3)	794 of 3 Dec 1992	Tasked with establishing a secure environment for humanitarian deliveries. Operated concurrently with UNOSOM I to secure delivery of humanitarian aid. The force was later partly absorbed into UNOSOM II.	37,000
Operation Deny Flight	Bosnia and Herzegovina (1993-5)	816 of 31 Mar 1993	NATO-led enforcement of Council-mandated no-fly zone; operated concurrently with UNPROFOR and its successor peacekeeping forces in the former Yugoslavia.	
Operation Turquoise	Rwanda (22 June-30 Sep 1994)	929 of 22 June 1994	French-led military intervention tasked with providing security for refugees and civilians. Followed, and operated concurrently with, UNAMIR peacekeeping force.	3,060
US-led Multinational Force (MNF)	Haiti (1994-5)	940 of 31 July 1994	Created conditions for the return of the elected government to Haiti. Followed, and operated concurrently with, UNMIH peacekeeping operation.	7,412 military personnel, 717 police
NATO-led Implementation Force (IFOR)	Bosnia and Herzegovina (1995-6)	1031 of 15 Dec 1995	Established following the Dayton peace agreement to bring an end to hostilities, separate forces, provide a safe and secure environment and support civilian implementation of the peace agreement.	c. 60,000

Name/description of operation	Location and duration	Authorising Security Council resolutions (UNSCRs)	Details	Strength
NATO-led Stabilisation Force (SFOR)	Bosnia and Herzegovina (1996–2004)	1088 of 12 Dec 1996	Followed IFOR, tasked with providing safe and secure environment in Bosnia, and supporting the International Criminal Tribunal and the Office of the High Representative (which oversaw the civilian implementation of the peace agreement).	c. 32,000
Inter-African Mission to Monitor the Implementation of the Bangui Agreements (MISAB)	Central African Republic (1997–8)	1125 of 6 Aug 1997	Originally established in February 1997 at the request of the government of the Central African Republic following army rebellions. The Security Council resolution of 6 August specified its task as restoring peace and security, in particular disarming rebels and militias. MISAB included forces from Burkina Faso, Chad, Gabon, Mali, Senegal and Togo.	c. 800
Italian-led Multinational Protection Force (MPF)	Albania (Apr–Aug 1997)	1101 of 28 Mar 1997	After the collapse of state institutions in Albania following the collapse of a government-run pyramid scheme, the Council authorised Italy to stabilise the situation to allow for elections, distribute humanitarian aid and establish control over Adriatic ports used for mass emigration to Italy.	6,294
NATO-led Kosovo Force (KFOR)	Kosovo (June 1999–)	1244 of 10 June 1999	Mandated to establish and maintain a safe and secure environment in Kosovo and to assist UNMIK.	c. 16,000 (Jan 2008)
Australian-led International Force for East Timor (INTERFET)	East Timor (Sep 1999– Feb 2000)	1264 of 15 Sep 1999	Preceded the establishment of, operated concurrently with and was later absorbed by UNTAET.	11,000
International Security Assistance Force (ISAF)	Afghanistan (Jan 2002–)	1386 of 20 Dec 2001	Established to assist the Afghan Transitional Authority and later the Afghan government in maintaining security within its area of responsibility. Led at first by individual NATO member countries and later by NATO.	c. 43,000 (Feb 2008)
Operation Licorne	Côte d'Ivoire (2003–)	1464 of 4 Feb 2003, 1528 of 27 Feb 2004	French forces (together with ECOWAS forces, see below) authorised to ensure the protection of civilians within their zones of operation. Since 2004, *Operation Licorne* forces have acted in support of the new UNOCI peacekeeping operation.	c. 4,600
ECOWAS Mission in Côte d'Ivoire (MICECI)	Côte d'Ivoire (2003–4)	1464 of 4 Feb 2003	ECOWAS forces (together with French forces of *Operation Licorne*) authorised to ensure the protection of civilians within their zones of operation. ECOWAS troops were 're-hatted' in 2004 to form part of the UNOCI peacekeeping operation.	c. 1,288
Operation Artemis	Ituri region of the DRC (15 June– 1 Sep 2003)	1484 of 30 May 2003	French-led EU force in support of UN peacekeeping operation MONUC; prepared the way for the Ituri Brigade peacekeepers deployed by MONUC.	c. 1,400

Name/description of operation	Location and duration	Authorising Security Council resolutions (UNSCRs)	Details	Strength
ECOWAS Multina-tional Force in Libe-ria (ECOMIL)	Liberia (4 Aug–1 Oct 2003)	1497 of 1 Aug 2003	ECOWAS force authorised to aid implementation of ceasefire agreement signed in Accra on 17 June 2003; prepared the way for deployment of UNMIL peacekeeping force.	c. 3,500–4,000 ECOWAS troops, plus 2,000 US Marines off the Liberian coast
US-led Multinational Force (MNF)	Iraq (2003–)	1511 of 16 Oct 2003	The Council authorised 'a multina-tional force under unified command to take all necessary measures to contribute to the maintenance of security and stability in Iraq'. Since then, the MNF has been the UN's official term for the US-led forces in Iraq.	c. 167,000 (Jan 2008)
US-led Multinational Interim Force (MIF)	Haiti (Mar–June 2004)	1529 of 29 Feb 2004	Paved way for MINUSTAH peacekeeping operation, transferring authority to it on 1 June 2004; certain MIF forces continued to operate in Haiti until 30 June 2004.	c. 3,800
African Union Mission in the Sudan (AMIS)	Darfur, Sudan (2004–7)	1556 of 30 July 2004	Invoking Chapter VII, the Council endorsed 'the deployment of international monitors, including the protection force envisioned by the African Union, to the Darfur region of Sudan under the leadership of the African Union'. AMIS was succeeded in 2007 by hybrid UN/African Union peacekeeping operation UNAMID.	4,657 military personnel, 608 military observers, 1,425 civilian police
European Union Force (EUFOR/ Operation Althea)	Bosnia and Herzegovina (2004–)	1575 of 22 Nov 2004	Succeeded SFOR in Bosnia and Herzegovina.	c. 2,200 (Feb 2008)
European Union Force (EUFOR RD Congo)	DRC (Apr–Nov 2006)	1671 of 25 Apr 2006	EU military mission deployed in support of MONUC peacekeeping force during the first democratic elections in the DRC in July and Aug 2006. Authorised for four months.	2,400
African Union Mission in Somalia (AMISOM)	Somalia (2007–)	1744 of 21 Feb 2007	African Union mission intended to stabilise Somalia after Ethiopian military intervention of Dec 2006, and to take the place of Ethiopian troops. Originally intended to remain in Somalia for six months, to be succeeded by a UN peacekeeping operation, but failure to find sufficient troops (Uganda has provided the only deployment to date) has meant that Ethiopian forces remain in Somalia.	c. 1,600 (Jan 2008)
European Union Force (EUFOR TCHAD/RCA)	Chad and Central African Republic (2008–)	1778 of 25 Sep 2007	Established to protect civilians and the delivery of humanitarian aid and to support MINURCAT peacekeeping operation in eastern Chad and the Central African Republic. Initially authorised for 12 months. Deployment was suspended in late 2007 due to rebel attacks on the Chadian capital, N'Djamena, but resumed in early 2008.	Up to 3,700

NOTES

Chapter One

1. Much emphasis has been placed on collective security in various works published throughout the UN's history. See for example Fernand van Langenhove, *La Crise du système de sécurité collective des Nations Unies 1946–57* (The Hague: Nijhoff, 1958); Jean Pierre Cot and Alain Pellet (eds), *La Charte des Nations Unies: Commentaire Article par Article* (Paris: Economica, 1985), pp. 7 & 75; and Bruno Simma (ed.), *The Charter of the United Nations: A Commentary*, 2nd ed. (Oxford: Oxford University Press, 2002), pp. 42, 760, 770.

2. This is a slight adaptation of the definition offered in Martin Wight, *Systems of States* (Leicester: Leicester University Press, 1977), p. 149.

3. Andreas Osiander, *The States System of Europe 1640–1990* (Oxford: Oxford University Press, 1994), pp. 40–3.

4. Wight, *Systems of States*, pp. 62 & 149–50.

5. In its discussion of the Security Council's powers in an advisory opinion of 20 July 1962 on 'Certain Expenses of the United Nations', the International Court of Justice stated that 'The responsibility conferred [by the Charter] is "primary", not exclusive.' *ICJ Reports 1962*, p. 163.

6. Charter of the United Nations, Article 27. The requirement that nine of the 15 Council members must vote for a resolution in order for it to pass was introduced in amendments that came into force on 31 August 1965. Before that date, an affirmative vote of seven members out of a total membership of 11 was needed.

7. UN General Assembly Resolution 377(V) A of 3 November 1950.

8. For a fuller account of the uses to which the 'Uniting for Peace' resolution has been put, see Dominik Zaum, 'The Security Council, the General Assembly and War: The Uniting for Peace Resolution', in Vaughan Lowe, Adam Roberts, Jennifer Welsh and Dominik Zaum (eds), *The United Nations Security Council and War: The Evolution of Thought and Practice since 1945* (Oxford: Oxford University Press, 2008), pp. 154–74. For a list of occasions on which the resolution has been invoked, see Appendix 6 of the same volume.

9. UN General Assembly Resolution ES–10/14 of 8 December 2003.

10. Edward C. Luck, 'A Council for All Seasons: The Creation of the Security Council and its Relevance for Today', in Lowe et al. (eds), *The United Nations Security Council and War: The Evolution of Thought and Practice since 1945*, pp. 61–85.

11. See Jennifer Welsh, 'The Security Council and Humanitarian Intervention', in Lowe et al. (eds), *The United Nations Security Council and War: The Evolution of Thought*

and Practice since 1945, pp. 535–62. A prominent example of Security Council involvement in the internal affairs of a state can be seen in the Council's deliberations over Haiti in UN Security Council Resolution (UNSCR) 841 of 16 June 1993. These were followed by a resolution authorising the use of force in Haiti – UNSCR 940 of 31 July 1994. The fact that large numbers of refugees had been fleeing Haiti had contributed to the country's situation being viewed as a threat to international peace and security.

12 UNSCR 1373 of 28 September 2001 and UNSCR 1566 of 8 October 2004 on threats to international peace and security caused by terrorist acts; and UNSCR 1540 of 28 April 2004 on nuclear non-proliferation.

13 UN Charter, Art. 42.

14 UN Charter, Arts 53 and 54.

15 Christine Gray, *International Law and the Use of Force*, 2nd edn (Oxford: Oxford University Press, 2004), pp. 282–327.

16 See UN General Assembly Resolution 60/1, '2005 World Summit Outcome', 16 September 2005, para. 177. By May 2008, the 'enemy state' provisions of the Charter had not been amended.

17 James Goodby, 'Can Collective Security Work? Reflections on the European Case', in Chester Crocker and Fen Osler Hampson (eds), *Managing Global Chaos: Sources of and Responses to International Conflict* (Washington DC: US Institute of Peace Press, 1996), p. 237. Goodby was special representative of the president for nuclear security and disarmament during the Clinton administration.

18 High-level Panel on Threats, Challenges and Change, *A More Secure World: Our Shared Responsibility – Report of the High-level Panel on Threats, Challenges and Change* (New York: United Nations, 2004), 'Synopsis', p. 1.

19 Peter Marshall, *Positive Diplomacy* (Basingstoke: Macmillan, 1997), p. 68.

20 'Report of the Panel on United Nations Peace Operations', UN document A/55/305 and S/2000/809 of 21 August 2000, p. ix.

21 Commonwealth of Independent States, an international organisation of 11 former Soviet republics.

22 UNSCR 1511 of 16 October 2003.

23 See UNSCR 1422 of 12 July 2002 and UNSCR 1423 of 12 July 2002.

24 Ilyana Kuziemko and Eric Werker, 'How Much is a Seat on the Security Council Worth? Foreign Aid and Bribery at the United Nations', *Journal of Political Economy*, vol. 114, no. 5, October 2006, pp. 905–30. Kuziemko and Werker's research on US aid to Security Council members encompasses the period 1946–2001.

25 UN General Assembly Resolution 1(I) of 24 January 1946, on 'Establishment of a Commission to Deal with the Problems Raised by the Discovery of Atomic Energy'. Although it was the General Assembly that established the commission specified by the resolution, the resolution directed that the new body was to report to the Security Council.

26 Treaty on the Non-Proliferation of Nuclear Weapons (1968), Art. X (3).

27 Richard Price, 'Nuclear Weapons Don't Kill People, Rogues Do', *International Politics*, vol. 44, nos 2–3, March–May 2007, pp. 232–49.

28 Jaswant Singh, 'Against Nuclear Apartheid', *Foreign Affairs*, vol. 77, no. 5, September–October 1998, p. 43.

29 Joachim Krause, 'Enlightenment and Nuclear Order', *International Affairs*, vol. 83, no. 3, May 2007, p. 498.

30 UNSCOM was created by UNSCR 687 of 3 April 1991; UNMOVIC by UNSCR 1284 of 17 December 1999. UNMOVIC's mandate was terminated by UNSCR 1762 of 29 June 2007.

31 The relevant resolutions are as follows: on Iraq, UNSCR 687; on North Korea, UNSCR 1718 of 14 October 2006; on Iran, UNSCR 1737 of 23 December 2006.

32 See UNSCR 1172 of 6 June 1998.

33 Samina Ahmed, 'Security Dilemmas of Nuclear-armed Pakistan', *Third World Quarterly*, vol. 21, no. 5, October 2000, p. 785; and the International Institute for Strategic Studies, *Nuclear Black*

Markets: Pakistan, A.Q. Khan and the rise of proliferation networks – A net assessment (London: IISS, 2007), pp. 25–6.

34 At the time of writing, divisions over the deal in the Indian coalition government between the Congress Party and the communists suggest that this agreement might fall through. See Edward Luce and Daniel Dombey, 'US–India Nuclear Deal Dead', FT.com, 11 June 2008.

35 For further details on the PSI, see Mark J. Valencia, *The Proliferation Security Initiative: Making waves in Asia*, Adelphi Paper 376 (Abingdon: Routledge for the IISS, 2005).

36 Erik Voeten, 'The Political Origins of the Security Council's Ability to Legitimize the Use of Force', *International Organization*, vol. 59, no. 3, Summer 2005, pp. 527–57.

37 For a more detailed discussion of the issue of Council non-involvement in conflicts, see John Dunbabin, 'The Security Council in the Wings: Exploring the Security Council's Non-Involvement in Wars', in Lowe et al. (eds), *The United Nations Security Council and War: The Evolution of Thought and Practice since 1945*, pp. 494–515.

38 Rahul Roy-Chaudhury, 'The Security Council and the India–Pakistan Wars', in Lowe et al. (eds), *The United Nations Security Council and War: The Evolution of Thought and Practice since 1945*, pp. 324–45.

39 Rupert Smith, 'The Security Council and the Bosnian Conflict: A Practitioner's View', in Lowe et al. (eds), *The United Nations Security Council and War: The Evolution of Thought and Practice since 1945*, p. 448.

40 See Roberts, 'Proposals for UN Standing Forces: A Critical History', in Lowe et al. (eds), *The United Nations Security Council and War: The Evolution of Thought and Practice since 1945*, p. 110.

41 UNSCR 1080 of 15 November 1996.

42 See Simon Chesterman, 'Does the UN have Intelligence?', *Survival*, vol. 48, no. 3, Autumn 2006, pp. 149–64.

Chapter Two

1 These include the difficulty of determining what distinguishes a war from other forms of political violence, the problems of comparing wars of differing length and intensity, the varying quality of data about casualties, the problems associated with comparing across different time periods, and the risks involved in extrapolating from past trends to the future.

2 Human Security Centre, *Human Security Report 2005: War and Peace in the 21st Century* (New York and Oxford: Oxford University Press, 2005), pp. 148–9.

3 For a classic short exposition of the possible security benefits of nuclear-weapons proliferation beyond the NPT-recognised powers, see Kenneth N. Waltz, *The Spread of Nuclear Weapons: More May Be Better*, Adelphi Paper 171 (London: IISS, 1981).

4 See Waltz, 'The Stability of a Bipolar World', *Daedalus*, vol. 93, no. 3, Summer 1964, pp. 881–909.

5 See John E. Mueller, *Retreat from Doomsday: The Obsolescence of Major War* (New York: Basic Books, 1990).

6 See Roberts, *Civil Resistance in the East European and Soviet Revolutions*, Einstein Institution Monograph Series no. 4 (Cambridge, MA: Albert Einstein Institution, 1991); and Adam Roberts and Timothy Garton Ash (eds), *Civil Resistance and Power Politics* (Oxford: Oxford University Press, forthcoming, 2009).

7 Roberts, 'The "War on Terror" in Historical Perspective', *Survival*, vol. 47, no. 2, Summer 2005, p. 103.

8   Respectively, UNSCR 748 of 31 March 1992; UNSCR 1054 of 26 April 1996; and UNSCR 1267 of 15 October 1999.

9   UNSCR 1373 of 28 September 2001.

10   For a detailed discussion of the Counter-Terrorism Committee and the wider efforts of the Security Council against terrorism, see Jane Boulden, 'The Security Council and Terrorism', in Lowe et al. (eds), *The United Nations Security Council and War: The Evolution of Thought and Practice since 1945*, pp. 608–23.

11   UNSCR 1566 of 8 October 2004.

12   UNSCR 1550 of 11 March 2004.

13   UN document S/13027 of 15 January 1979.

14   Brian McCauley, 'Hungary and Suez, 1956: The Limits of Soviet and American Power', *Journal of Contemporary History*, vol. 16, no. 4, October 1981, p. 790. In the Security Council debate on Hungary of 3 November 1956, the US abstained from a motion to extend the time allotted to the debate, and then voted against a motion to resume discussion of the issue the following day. See McCauley, 'Hungary and Suez, 1956: The Limits of Soviet and American Power', p. 794.

15   Charles Tripp, 'The Security Council and the Iran–Iraq War', in Lowe et al. (eds), *The United Nations Security Council and War: The Evolution of Thought and Practice since 1945*, pp. 368–83.

16   'Further Report of the Secretary-General on the Implementation of Security Council Resolution 598, 1987', UN document S/23273 of 9 December 1991.

17   Constitutive Act of the African Union (2002), Article 4 (h). Available at http://www.africa-union.org.

18   Such concern on the part of involved governments about the effect of a General Assembly ceasefire resolution was evident during the Suez crisis of October–November 1956. See for example, on Israeli attitudes, Maj.-Gen. Moshe Dayan, *Diary of the Sinai Campaign* (London: Weidenfeld & Nicolson, 1966), pp. 27–9; and on Anglo-French attitudes, Anthony Nutting, *No End of a Lesson: The Story of Suez* (London: Constable, 1967), pp. 131–5.

19   When it signed the Lomé agreement on 7 July 1999, the UN added a reservation stating that, for the UN, the amnesty could not cover crimes of genocide, crimes against humanity, war crimes and other serious violations of international humanitarian law. See 'Report of the Secretary-General on the United Nations Observer Mission in Sierra Leone', UN document S/1999/836 of 30 July 1999, para. 7.

20   On the rationale for the CIS peacekeeping force, see the letter from the Permanent Representative of the Russian Federation to the UN Secretary-General, UN document S/1994/732 of 21 June 1994. From the start, the CIS force operated in coordination with the much smaller UN Observer Mission in Georgia.

21   Catherine Dale, 'The Case of Abkhazia (Georgia)', in Lena Jonson and Clive Archer (eds), *Peacekeeping and the Role of Russia in Eurasia* (Boulder, CO: Westview, 1996), pp. 121–37.

22   The UN's and UNAMSIL's objectives in Sierra Leone had been set out in UNSCR 1289 of 7 February 2000. UNAMSIL had proved ineffective in carrying out key parts of its mission in the intervening time.

23   No such enforcement operation has in fact ever been established, and, as successive Secretaries-General have stated since the end of the Cold War, the UN lacks the capacity to mount such an operation. See Boutros Boutros-Ghali, 'Supplement to an Agenda for Peace: Position Paper of the Secretary-General on the Occasion of the Fiftieth Anniversary of the United Nations', UN document A/50/60 of 3 January 1995, paras 77–8; Kofi Annan, 'Renewing the United Nations: A Programme for Reform', UN document A/51/950 of 14 July 1997, para. 107.

Chapter Three

1   This chapter draws on Adam Roberts, 'Proposals for UN Standing Forces: A Critical History', in Lowe et al. (eds), *The United Nations Security Council and War: The Evolution of Thought and Practice since 1945*, pp. 99–130.

2   'General Principles Governing the Organization of the Armed Forces Made Available to the Security Council by Member Nations of the United Nations: Report of the Military Staff Committee', UN document S/336 of 30 April 1947. For an account of UN discussions from 1946–8, drawn from British archives, see Eric Grove, 'UN Armed Forces and the Military Staff Committee', *International Security*, vol. 17, no. 4, Spring 1993, pp. 172–82.

3   Trygve Lie, *In the Cause of Peace: Seven Years with the United Nations* (New York: Macmillan, 1954), p. 98.

4   Andrew Cordier and Wilder Foote (eds), *Public Papers of the Secretaries-General of the United Nations*, Volume I, *Trygve Lie, 1946–1953* (New York: Columbia University Press, 1969), p. 186.

5   'Second Report of the Collective Measures Committee', General Assembly Official Records, 7th session, Supplement 17, October 1952, p. 12. General Assembly Resolution 703 of 17 March 1953, under which the report was formally accepted, made no mention of the Legion or Volunteer Reserve proposals.

6   William R. Frye, *A United Nations Peace Force* (New York: Oceana, 1957). See also the appendix, by Stephen Schwebel, on Trygve Lie's proposals for a UN Guard and UN Legion.

7   Grenville Clark and Louis B. Sohn, *World Peace Through World Law* (Cambridge, MA: Harvard University Press, 1958), p. 300.

8   'Stand-by Arrangements for Peacekeeping: Report of the Secretary-General', UN document S/1994/777 of 30 June 1994, para. 2. This short document conveys an air of scepticism about the adequacy of such arrangements.

Chapter Four

1   See for example two accounts based on close knowledge of the UN in the early 1990s. Marrack Goulding, *Peacemonger* (London: John Murray, 2002), by the UN Under-Secretary-General in charge of peacekeeping up to March 1993, is explicit on the impossible workload and consequent decline in performance (p. 138); David Hannay, *New World Disorder: The UN After the Cold War – An Insider's View* (London: I.B. Tauris, 2008), by the UK Permanent Representative to the UN, 1990–95, comments on 'the sheer fecklessness with which the member states piled new tasks onto the UN, new peace operations, new responsibilities in the fields of the environment, of health, of criminal justice, without pausing to consider how the human and financial resources needed to carry them out were to be provided' (p. 292).

2   Mats Berdal, 'The Security Council and Peacekeeping', in Lowe et al. (eds), *The United Nations Security Council and War: The Evolution of Thought and Practice since 1945*, p. 190.

3   This section draws on Richard Caplan, 'The Security Council and the Administration of War-Torn and Contested Territories', in Lowe et al. (eds), *The United Nations Security Council and War: The Evolution of Thought and Practice since 1945*, pp. 563–79.

4 For UNMIK's mandate, see UNSCR 1244 of 10 June 1999; for UNTAET's, see UNSCR 1272 of 25 October 1999.

5 Since the independence of the last trust territory, Palau, in 1994, the Trusteeship Council has been dormant, and at the 2005 World Summit, member states decided that the relevant sections of Chapters XII and XIII should be deleted from the Charter. By May 2008, no changes had been made. See General Assembly Resolution 60/1, '2005 World Summit Outcome', para. 176.

6 UNSCR 1037 of 15 January 1996.

7 For a detailed discussion of the international administration of Kosovo and East Timor, see Zaum, *The Sovereignty Paradox: The Norms and Politics of International Statebuilding* (Oxford: Oxford University Press, 2007).

8 See Roberts, 'The So-Called "Right" of Humanitarian Intervention', *Yearbook of International Humanitarian Law: Vol. 3, 2000* (The Hague: T.M.C. Asser Press, 2002), pp. 22–3; and Roy-Chaudhury, 'The Security Council and the India–Pakistan Wars', p. 339.

9 Emma Rothschild, 'What is Security?', *Daedalus*, vol. 124, no. 3, Summer 1995, pp. 53–98.

10 Report of the International Commission on Intervention and State Sovereignty, *The Responsibility to Protect* (Ottawa: International Development Research Centre, December 2001).

11 For a detailed discussion of such authorisations, see Jennifer M. Welsh, 'The Security Council and Humanitarian Intervention', in Lowe et al. (eds), *The United Nations Security Council and War: The Evolution of Thought and Practice since 1945*, pp. 535–62.

12 See UNSCR 1373 of 28 September 2001. See also Paul Szasz, 'The Security Council Starts Legislating', *American Journal of International Law*, vol. 97, no. 4, Autumn 2003, pp. 901–2.

13 See in particular the statement of Pakistan, speaking on behalf of the G77 in the Security Council debate on climate change. UN document S/PV.5663 of 17 April 2007, pp. 24–5, available at http://unbisnet.un.org.

14 This section draws on Georg Nolte, 'The Different Functions of the Security Council with Respect to Humanitarian Law', in Lowe et al. (eds), *The United Nations Security Council and War: The Evolution of Thought and Practice since 1945*, pp. 519–34.

15 *Ibid.*, p. 520.

16 UNSCR 1265 of 17 September 1999; UNSCR 1296 of 19 April 2000; UNSCR 1674 of 28 April 2006; and UNSCR 1738 of 23 December 2006.

17 For the sanctions on Sudan, see UNSCR 1591 of 29 March 2005 and UNSCR 1672 of 25 April 2006; for those on the DRC, see UNSCR 1649 of 21 December 2005.

18 See Rachel Kerr, *The International Criminal Tribunal for the Former Yugoslavia: An Exercise in Law, Politics, and Diplomacy* (Oxford: Oxford University Press, 2004); Virginia Morris and Michael P. Scharf, *The International Criminal Tribunal for Rwanda* (Irvington-on-Hudson, NY: Transnational Publishers, 1998); and Cesare P.R. Romano, André Nollkaemper and Jann K. Kleffner, *Internationalized Criminal Courts and Tribunals: Sierra Leone, East Timor, Kosovo and Cambodia* (Oxford: Oxford University Press, 2004). For the Lebanon tribunal, see note 19.

19 On the genesis of one of the later tribunals, see 'Report of the Secretary-General on the Establishment of a Special Tribunal for Lebanon', UN document S/2006/893 of 15 November 2006.

20 See Jeremy Greenstock, 'The Security Council in the Post-Cold War World', in Lowe et al. (eds), *The United Nations Security Council and War: The Evolution of Thought and Practice since 1945*, pp. 255–6. Reports of many Security Council missions can be found at www.un.org/docs/sc/missionreports.html.

21 On the evolving structure of Council committees in general, and the Counter-Terrorism Committee in particular, see Boulden, 'The Security Council and Terrorism', pp. 613–18.

Chapter Five

1. This section draws on the contribution of Sir Frank Berman to the introduction of Lowe et al. (eds), *The United Nations Security Council and War: The Evolution of Thought and Practice since 1945*, pp. 39–43.

2. For a discussion of accountability and the Security Council, see Ruth W. Grant and Robert O. Keohane, 'Accountability and Abuses of Power in World Politics', IILJ Working Paper 2004/7, 2004, Global Administrative Law Series, Institute for International Law and Justice, New York University School of Law, http://iilj.org/publications/2004-7Keohans.asp. See also International Law Association, 'Report of the 71st Conference, Berlin, 2004', pp. 164–234.

3. UNSCR 678 of 29 November 1990.

4. Goulding, *Peacemonger*, pp. 340–1.

5. In 1993, the General Assembly established the Open-Ended Working Group on the Question of Equitable Representation of and an Increase in the Membership of the Security Council. The group's work was summarised in a 1997 proposal from the then-General Assembly President Razali Ismail, which still serves as a basis for reform discussions. For further discussion of pre-2005 reform negotiations, see Mark Zacher, 'The Conundrums of International Power Sharing: The Politics of Security Council Reform', in Richard Price and Mark Zacher (eds), *The United Nations and Global Security* (New York: Palgrave, 2004), pp. 211–25.

6. Report of the Secretary-General, 'In Larger Freedom: Towards Security, Development and Human Rights for All', UN document A/59/2005 of 21 March 2005, paras 165–83.

7. See General Assembly Resolution 60/1, '2005 World Summit Outcome', paras 152–4.

8. Edward C. Luck, 'The UN Security Council: Reform or Enlarge?', in Paul Heinbecker and Patricia Goff (eds), *Irrelevant or Indispensable? The United Nations in the 21st Century* (Waterloo, ON: Wilfred Laurier University Press, 2005), pp. 143–52.

9. *Ibid.*, pp. 151–2.

10. Jochen Prantl, 'Informal Groups of States and the UN Security Council', *International Organization*, vol. 59, no. 3, Summer 2005, p. 584.

11. In UNSCR 1353 of 13 June 2001, the Council committed itself to involving troop contributors in discussions of mandates, in accordance with Article 44 of the UN Charter.

12. For detailed discussions of these reforms, see Susan C. Hulton, 'Council Working Methods and Procedure', in David Malone (ed.), *The UN Security Council: From the Cold War to the 21st Century* (Boulder, CO: Lynne Rienner, 2004), pp. 237–51; and Security Council Report, 'Security Council Transparency, Legitimacy and Effectiveness: Efforts to Reform Council Working Methods 1993–2007', Special Research Report, 18 October 2007, http://www.securitycouncilreport.org/atf/cf/%7B65BFCF9B-6D27-4E9C-8CD3-CF6E4FF96FF9%7D/Research%20Report_Working%20Methods%2018%20Oct%2007.pdf.

13. General Assembly Resolution 60/1, '2005 World Summit Outcome', para. 154.

14. G. John Ikenberry and Anne-Marie Slaughter, Final Report of the Princeton Project on National Security, *Forging a World of Liberty Under Law: US National Security in the 21st Century*, Princeton Project Papers (Princeton, NJ: Woodrow Wilson School of Public and International Affairs, 27 September 2006), p. 61.

15. John McCain, 'America Must be a Good Role Model', *Financial Times*, 18 March 2008.

Conclusion

1   International Commission on Intervention and State Sovereignty, *The Responsibility to Protect*, p. xii.

2   Ian Hurd, 'Legitimacy, Power, and the Symbolic Life of the UN Security Council', *Global Governance*, vol. 8, no.1, January–March 2002, p. 35.

3   See Simon Chesterman, *Shared Secrets: Intelligence and Collective Security*, Lowy Institute Paper 10 (Sydney: Lowy Institute for International Policy, 2006).

4   See Paul A. Volcker, Richard J. Goldstone and Mark Pieth, Report of the Independent Inquiry Committee into the UN Oil-for-Food Programme, *The Management of the United Nations Oil-for-Food Programme*, 7 September 2005. One of a series of five major reports of the Independent Inquiry Committee into the UN Oil-for-Food Programme chaired by Volcker, this report stated (on pp. 2–5) that the UN needed stronger executive leadership and major administrative reform; also that the members of the Security Council must shoulder their share of the blame for the uneven and wavering direction of the programme.

5   See Hans Kundnani, 'Compass Settles Claims of Bribery in UN Contracts', *Guardian*, 17 October 2006, p. 27.

6   The problem of sexual abuse and exploitation by blue helmets surfaced in 2004. In 2005, a UN report stated that a 'shockingly large number' of peacekeepers had engaged in such practices in the DRC, with payments for sex ranging from two eggs to $5 per encounter. Among the victims, who were often illiterate, were many abandoned orphans. Representatives of the UN and several NGOs (there were also allegations against NGO aid workers) responded to the scandal with a 'Statement of Commitment on Eliminating Sexual Exploitation and Abuse by UN and Non-UN Personnel' http://www.un.org/Depts/dpko/CDT/statement.pdf, and investigative and disciplinary action was taken. By the end of November 2006, 319 UN peacekeeping personnel from a range of missions had been investigated. The probes resulted in the summary dismissal of 18 civilians and the repatriation on disciplinary grounds of 17 police and 144 military personnel. See the letter from UN Under-Secretary-General for Peacekeeping Operations Jean-Marie Guéhenno to the *Independent*, 9 January 2007, http://www.un.org/Depts/dpko/dpko/ctte/jmg2.pdf.

7   Inis L. Claude, Jr, 'Collective Legitimization as a Political Function of the United Nations', *International Organization*, vol. 20, no. 3, Summer 1966, pp. 367–79.

8   The Just War tradition dates back at least to St Augustine. A modern treatment can be found in Michael Walzer, *Just and Unjust Wars: A Moral Argument with Historical Illustrations*, 3rd ed. (New York: Basic Books, 2000). The other principles usually associated with the tradition are just cause, right intention, last resort, reasonable prospects of success and proportionality.

9   Legitimate authority to authorise the use of force, including that of the UN Security Council, is discussed in some of the contributions to Charles Reed and David Ryall (eds), *The Price of Peace: Just War in the Twenty-First Century* (Cambridge: Cambridge University Press, 2007), esp. Frank Berman (pp. 162–9), Michael Quinlan (pp. 292–3) and Richard Harries (pp. 305–6).

10   Claude, 'Collective Legitimization as a Political Function of the United Nations', p. 374.

11   Michael W. Doyle and Nicholas Sambanis, *Making War and Building Peace: United Nations Peace Operations* (Princeton, NJ: Princeton University Press, 2006).

Appendix

[1]   This appendix is a modified and updated version of Appendix 3 in Lowe et al. (eds), *The United Nations Security Council and War: The Evolution of Thought and Practice since 1945* (Oxford: Oxford University Press, 2008), pp. 672–7.

⌐IISS ADELPHI PAPERS

RECENT **ADELPHI PAPERS** INCLUDE:

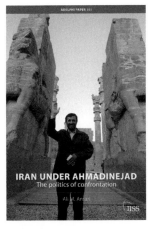

ADELPHI PAPER 393

Iran under Ahmadinejad: The politics of confrontation

Ali M. Ansari

ISBN 978-0-415-45486-5

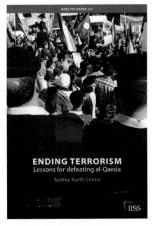

ADELPHI PAPER 394

Ending Terrorism: Lessons for defeating al-Qaeda

Audrey Kurth Cronin

ISBN 978-0-415-45062-1

All Adelphi Papers are £15.99 / $28.95

For credit card orders call **+44 (0) 1264 343 071**
or e-mail **book.orders@tandf.co.uk**

The Evolution of Strategic Thought
Classic Adelphi Papers

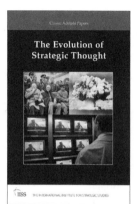

The Adelphi Papers monograph series is the Institute's principal contribution to policy-relevant, original academic research. Collected on the occasion of the Institute's 50th anniversary, the twelve Adelphi Papers in this volume represent some of the finest examples of writing on strategic issues. They offer insights into the changing security landscape of the past half-century and glimpses of some of the most significant security events and trends of our times, from the Cold War nuclear arms race, through the oil crisis of 1973, to the contemporary challenge of asymmetric war in Iraq and Afghanistan.

Published April 2008; 704 pp.

Bookpoint Ltd. 130 Milton Park, Abingdon, Oxon OX14 4SB, UK
Tel: +44 (0)1235 400524, Fax: +44 (0)1235 400525
Customer orders: book.orders@tandf.co.uk
Bookshops, wholesalers and agents:
Email (UK): uktrade@tandf.co.uk,
email (international): international@tandf.co.uk

Routledge
Taylor & Francis Group

ⓘISS THE INTERNATIONAL INSTITUTE FOR STRATEGIC STUDIES